Strange Pages fror Papers

T. F. Thiselton-Dyer

Alpha Editions

This edition published in 2024

ISBN : 9789362994769

Design and Setting By
Alpha Editions
www.alphaedis.com
Email - info@alphaedis.com

As per information held with us this book is in Public Domain.
This book is a reproduction of an important historical work. Alpha Editions uses the best technology to reproduce historical work in the same manner it was first published to preserve its original nature. Any marks or number seen are left intentionally to preserve its true form.

Contents

CHAPTER I. FATAL CURSES. .... - 1 -

CHAPTER II. THE SCREAMING SKULL. .... - 15 -

CHAPTER III. ECCENTRIC VOWS. .... - 24 -

CHAPTER IV. STRANGE BANQUETS. .... - 36 -

CHAPTER V. MYSTERIOUS ROOMS. .... - 46 -

CHAPTER VI. INDELIBLE BLOOD STAINS. .... - 59 -

CHAPTER VII. CURIOUS SECRETS. .... - 70 -

CHAPTER VIII. THE DEAD HAND. .... - 81 -

CHAPTER IX. DEVIL COMPACTS. .... - 85 -

CHAPTER X. FAMILY DEATH OMENS. .... - 94 -

CHAPTER XI. WEIRD POSSESSIONS. .... - 104 -

CHAPTER XII. ROMANCE OF DISGUISE. .... - 109 -

CHAPTER XIII. EXTRAORDINARY DISAPPEARANCES. .... - 121 -

CHAPTER XIV. HONOURED HEARTS. .... - 134 -

CHAPTER XV. ROMANCE OF WEALTH. ....- 139 -

CHAPTER XVI. LUCKY ACCIDENTS. ....- 148 -

CHAPTER XVII. FATAL PASSION. ....- 153 -

CHAPTER I.
FATAL CURSES.

> May the grass wither from thy feet! the woods
> Deny thee shelter! Earth a home! the dust
> A grave! The sun his light! and heaven her God.
>
> BYRON, Cain.

Many a strange and curious romance has been handed down in the history of our great families, relative to the terrible curses uttered in cases of dire extremity against persons considered guilty of injustice and wrong doing. It is to such fearful imprecations that the misfortune and downfall of certain houses have been attributed, although, it may be, centuries have elapsed before their final fulfilment. Such curses, too, unlike the fatal "Curse of Kehama," have rarely turned into blessings, nor have they been thought to be as harmless as the curse of the Cardinal-Archbishop of Rheims, who banned the thief—both body and soul, his life and for ever—who stole his ring. It was an awful curse, but none of the guests seemed the worse for it, except the poor jackdaw who had hidden the ring in some sly corner as a practical joke. But, if we are to believe traditionary and historical lore, only too many of the curses recorded in the chronicles of family history have been productive of the most disastrous results, reminding us of that dreadful malediction given by Byron in his "Curse of Minerva":

"So let him stand, through ages yet unborn,Fix'd statue on the pedestal of scorn."

A popular form of curse seems to have been the gradual collapse of the family name from failure of male-issue; and although there is, perhaps, no more romantic chapter in the vicissitudes of many a great house than its final extinction from lack of an heir, such a disaster is all the more to be lamented when resulting from a curse. A catastrophe of this kind was that connected with the M'Alister family of Scotch notoriety. The story goes that many generations back, one of their chiefs, M'Alister Indre—an intrepid warrior who feared neither God nor man—in a skirmish with a neighbouring clan, captured a widow's two sons, and in a most heartless manner caused them to be hanged on a gibbet erected almost before her very door. It was in vain that, with well nigh heartbroken tears, she denounced his iniquitous act, for his comrades and himself only laughed and scoffed, and even threatened to burn her cottage to the ground. But as the crimson and setting rays of a summer sun fell on the lifeless bodies of her two sons, her eyes met those of him who had so basely and cruelly wronged her, and, after once more stigmatizing his barbarity, with deep measured voice she pronounced these ominous words, embodying a curse which M'Alister Indre little anticipated would so surely come to pass. "I suffer now," said the grief-stricken woman, "but you shall suffer always—you have made me childless, but you and yours shall be heirless for ever—never shall there be a son to the house of M'Alister."

These words were treated with contempt by M'Alister Indre, who mocked and laughed at the malicious prattle of a woman's tongue. But time proved only too truly how persistently the curse of the bereaved woman clung to the race of her oppressors, and, as Sir Bernard Burke remarks, it was in the reign of Queen Anne that the hopes of the house of M'Alister "flourished for the last time, they were blighted for ever." The closing scene of this prophetic curse was equally tragic and romantic; for, whilst espousing the cause of the Pretender, the young and promising heir of the M'Alisters was taken prisoner, and with many others put to death. Incensed at the wrongs of his exiled monarch, and full of fiery impulse, he had secretly left his youthful wife, and joined the army at Perth that was to restore the Pretender to his throne. For several months the deserted wife fretted under the terrible suspense, often silently wondering if, after all, her husband—the last hope of the House of M'Alister—was to fall under the ban of the widow's curse. She could not dispel from her mind the hitherto disastrous results of those ill-fated words, and would only too willingly have done anything in her power to make atonement for the wrong that had been committed in the past. It was whilst almost frenzied with thoughts of this distracting kind, that vague rumours reached her ears of a great battle which had been fought, and ere long this was followed by the news that the Pretender's forces had been successful, and that he was about to be crowned at Scone. The shades of evening were fast setting in as, overcome with the joyous prospect of seeing her husband home again, she withdrew to her chamber, and, flinging herself on her bed in a state of hysteric delight, fell asleep. But her slumbers were broken, for at every sound she started, mentally exclaiming "Can that be my husband?"

At last, the happy moment came when her poor overwrought brain made sure it heard his footsteps. She listened, yes! they were his! Full of feverish joy she was longing to see that long absent face, when, as the door opened, to her horror and dismay, there entered a figure in martial array without a head. It was enough—he was dead. And with an agonizing scream she fell down in a swoon; and on becoming conscious only lived to hear the true narrative of the battle of Sheriff-Muir, which had brought to pass the Widow's Curse that there should be no heir to the house of M'Alister.

This story reminds us of one told of Sir Richard Herbert, who, with his brother, the Earl of Pembroke, pursuing a robber band in Anglesea, had captured seven brothers, the ringleaders of "many mischiefs and murders." The Earl of Pembroke determined to make an example of these marauders, and, to root out so wretched a progeny, ordered them all to be hanged. Upon this, the mother of the felons came to the Earl of Pembroke, and upon her knees besought him to pardon two, or at least one, of her sons, a request which was seconded by the Earl's brother, Sir Richard. But the Earl, finding the condemned men all equally guilty, declared he could make no distinction, and ordered them to be hanged together.

Upon this the mother, falling upon her knees, cursed the Earl, and prayed that God's mischief might fall upon him in the first battle in which he was engaged. Curious to relate, on the eve of the battle of Edgcot Field, having marshalled his men in order to fight, the Earl of Pembroke was surprised to find his brother, Sir Richard Herbert, standing in the front of his company, and leaning upon his pole-axe in a most dejected and pensive mood.

"What," cried the Earl, "doth thy great body" (for Sir Richard was taller than anyone in the army) "apprehend anything, that thou art so melancholy? or art thou weary with marching, that thou dost lean thus upon thy pole-axe?"

"I am not weary with marching," replied Sir Richard, "nor do I apprehend anything for myself; but I cannot but apprehend on your part lest the curse of the woman fall upon you."

And the curse of the frantic mother of seven convicts seemed, we are told, to have gained the authority of Heaven, for both the Earl and his brother Sir Richard, were defeated at the battle of Edgcot, were both taken prisoners and put to death.

Sir Walter Scott has made a similar legend the subject of one of his ballads in the "Minstrelsy of the Scottish Border," entitled "The Curse of Moy," a tale founded on an ancient Highland tradition that originated in a feud between the clans of Chattan and Grant. The Castle of Moy, the early residence of Mackintosh, the chief of the clan Chattan, is situated among the mountains of Inverness-shire, and stands on the edge of a small gloomy lake called Loch Moy, in which is still shown a rocky island as the spot where the dungeon stood in which prisoners were confined by the former chiefs of Moy. On a certain evening, in the annals of Moy, the scene is represented as having been one of extreme merriment, for

In childbed lay the lady fair,But now is come the appointed hour.And vassals shout, "An heir, an heir!"

It is no ordinary occasion, for a wretched curse has long hung over the Castle of Moy, but at last the spell seems broken, and, as the well-spiced bowl goes round, shout after shout echoes and re-echoes through the castle, "An heir, an heir!" Many a year had passed without the prospect of such an event, and it had looked as if the ill-omened words uttered in the past were to be realised. It was no wonder then that "in the gloomy towers of Moy" there were feasting and revelry, for a child is born who is to perpetuate the clan which hitherto had seemed threatened with extinction. But, even on this festive night when every heart is tuned for song and mirth, there suddenly appears a mysterious figure, a pale and shivering form, by "age and frenzy haggard made," who defiantly exclaims "'Tis vain! 'Tis vain!"

At once all eyes are turned on this strange form, as she, in mocking gesture, casts a look of withering scorn on the scene around her, and startles the jovial vassals with the reproachful words "No heir! No heir!" The laughter is hushed, the pipes no longer sound, for the witch with uplifted hand beckons that she had a message to tell—a message from Death—she might truly say, "What means these bowls of wine—these festive songs?"

For the blast of Death is on the heath,And the grave yawns wide for the child of Moy.

She then recounts the tale of treachery and cruelty committed by a chief of the House of Moy in the days of old, for which "his name shall perish for ever off the earth—a son may be born—but that son shall verily die." The witch brings tears into many an eye as she tells how this curse was uttered by one Margaret, a prominent figure in this sad feud, for it was when deceived in the most base manner, and when betrayed by a man who had violated his promise he had solemnly pledged, that she is moved to pronounce the fatal words of doom:

She pray'd that childless and forlorn,The chief of Moy might pine away,That the sleepless night, and the careful mornMight wither his limbs in slow decay.

But never the son of a chief of MoyMight live to protect his father's age,Or close in peace his dying eye,Or gather his gloomy heritage.

Such was the "Curse of Moy," uttered, it must be remembered, too, by a fair young girl, against the Chief of Moy for a blood-thirsty crime—the act of a traitor—in that, not content with slaying her father, and murdering her lover, he satiates his brutal passion by letting her eyes rest on their corpses.

"And here," they said, "is thy father dead, And thy lover's corpse is cold at his side."

Her tale ended, the witch departs, but now ceased the revels of the shuddering clan, for "despair had seized on every breast," and "in every vein chill terror ran." On the morrow, all is changed, no joyous sounds are heard, but silence reigns supreme—the silence of death. The curse has triumphed, the last hope of the house of Moy is gone, and—

Scarce shone the morn on the mountain's head When the lady wept o'er her dying boy.

But tyranny, or oppression, has always been supposed to bring its own punishment, as in the case of Barcroft Hall, Lancashire, where the "Idiot's Curse" is commonly said to have caused the downfall of the family. The tradition current in the neighbourhood states that one of the heirs to Barcroft was of weak intellect, and that he was fastened by a younger brother with a chain in one of the cellars, and there in a most cruel manner gradually starved to death. It appears that this unnatural conduct on the part of the younger brother was prompted by a desire to get possession of the property; and it is added that, long before the heir to Barcroft was released from his sufferings, he caused a report to be circulated that he was dead, and by this piece of deception made himself master of the Barcroft estate. It was in one of his lucid intervals that the poor injured brother pronounced a curse upon the family of the Barcrofts, to the effect that their name should perish for ever, and that the property should pass into other hands. But this malediction was only regarded as the ravings of an imbecile, unaccountable for his words, and little or no heed was paid to this death sentence on the Barcroft name. And yet, light as the family made of it, within a short time there were not wanting indications that their prosperity was on the wane, a fact which every year became more and more discernible until the curse was fulfilled in the person of Thomas Barcroft, who died in 1688 without male issue. After passing through the hands of the Bradshaws, the Pimlots, and the Isherwoods, the property was finally sold to Charles Towneley, the celebrated antiquarian, in the year 1795.[1] Whatever the truth of this family tradition, Barcroft is still a good specimen of the later Tudor style, and its ample cellarage gives an idea of the profuse hospitality of its former owners, some rude scribblings on one of the walls of which are still pointed out as the work of the captive.

In a still more striking way this spirit of persecution incurred its own condemnation. In the 17th century, Francis Howgill, a noted Quaker, travelled about the South of England preaching, which at Bristol was the cause of serious rioting. On returning to his own neighbourhood, he was summoned to appear before the justices who were holding a court in a tavern at Kendal, and, on his refusing to take the oath of allegiance, he was imprisoned in Appleby Gaol. In due time, the judges of assizes tendered the same oath, but with the like result, and evidently wishing to show him some consideration offered to release him from custody if he would give a bond for his good behaviour in the interim, which likewise declining to do, he was recommitted to prison. In the course of his imprisonment, however, a curious incident happened, which gave rise to the present narrative. Having been permitted by the magistrates to go home to Grayrigg for a few days on private affairs, he took the opportunity of calling on a justice of the name of Duckett, residing at Grayrigg Hall, who was not only a great persecutor of the Quakers but was one of the magistrates who had committed him to prison. As might be imagined, Justice Duckett was not a little surprised at seeing Howgill, and said to him, "What is your wish now, Francis? I thought you had been in Appleby Gaol."

Howgill, keenly resenting the magistrate's behaviour, promptly replied, "No, I am not, but I am come with a message from the Lord. Thou hast persecuted the Lord's people, but His hand is now against thee, and He will send a blast upon all that thou hast, and thy name shall rot out of the earth, and this thy dwelling shall become desolate, and a habitation for owls and jackdaws." When Howgill had delivered his message, the magistrate seems to have been somewhat disconcerted, and said, "Francis, are you in earnest?" But Howgill only added, "Yes, I am in earnest, it is the word of the Lord to thee, and there are many living now who will see it."

But the most remarkable part of the story remains to be told. By a strange coincidence the prophetic utterance of Howgill was fulfilled in a striking manner, for all the children of Justice Duckett died without leaving any issue, whilst some of them came to actual poverty, one begging her bread from door to door. Grayrigg Hall passed into the possession of the Lowther family, was dismantled, and fell into ruins, little more than its extensive foundations being visible in 1777, and, after having long been the habitation of "owls and jackdaws," the ruins were entirely removed and a farmhouse erected upon the site of the "old hall," in accordance with what was popularly known as "The Quaker's Curse, and its fulfilment." Cornish biography, however, tells how a magistrate of that county, Sir John Arundell, a man greatly esteemed amongst his neighbours for his honourable conduct—fell under an imprecation which he in no way deserved. In his official capacity, it seems, he had given offence to a shepherd who had by some means acquired considerable influence over the peasantry, under the impression that he possessed some supernatural powers. This man, for some offence, had been imprisoned by Sir John Arundell, and on his release would constantly waylay the magistrate, always looking at him with the same menacing eye, at the same time slowly muttering these words:

"When upon the yellow sand, Thou shalt die by human hand."

Notwithstanding Sir John Arundell's education and position, he was not wholly free from the superstition of the period, and might have thought, too, that this man intended to murder him. Hence he left his home at Efford and retired to the wood-clad hills of Trevice, where he lived for some years without the annoyance of meeting his old enemy. But in the tenth year of Edward IV., Richard de Vere, Earl of Oxford, seized St. Michael's Mount; on hearing of which news, Sir John Arundell, then Sheriff of Cornwall—led an attack on St. Michael's Mount, in the course of which he received his death wound in a skirmish on the sands near Marazion. Although he had broken up his home at Efford "to counteract the will of fate," the shepherd's prophecy was accomplished; and tradition even says that, in his dying moments, his old enemy appeared, singing in joyous tones:

"When upon the yellow sand, Thou shalt die by human hand."

The misappropriation of property, in addition to causing many a family complication, has occasionally been attended with a far more serious result. There is a strange curse, for instance, in the family of Mar, which can boast of great antiquity, there being, perhaps, no title in Europe so ancient as that of the Earl of Mar. This curse has been attributed by some to Thomas the Rhymer, by others to the Abbot of Cambuskenneth, and by others to the Bard of the House at that epoch. But, whoever its author, the curse was delivered prior to the elevation of the Earl, in the year 1571, to be the Regent of Scotland, and runs thus:

"Proud Chief of Mar, thou shalt be raised still higher, until thou sittest in the place of the King. Thou shalt rule and destroy, and thy work shall be after thy name, but thy work shall be the emblem of thy house, and shall teach mankind that he who cruelly and haughtily raiseth himself upon the ruins of the holy cannot prosper. Thy work shall be cursed, and shall never be finished. But thou shalt have riches and greatness, and shall be true to thy sovereign, and shalt raise his banner in the field of blood. Then, when thou seemest to be highest, when thy power is mightiest, then shall come thy fall; low shall be thy head amongst the nobles of the people. Deep shall be thy moan among the children of dool (sorrow). Thy lands shall be given to the stranger, and thy titles shall lie among the dead. The branch that springs from thee shall see his dwelling burnt, in which a King is nursed—his wife a sacrifice in that same flame; his children numerous, but of little honour; and three born and grown who shall never see the light. Yet shall thine ancient tower stand; for the brave and the true cannot be wholly forsaken. Thou, proud head and daggered hand, must dree thy weird, until horses shall be stabled in thy hall, and a weaver shall throw his shuttle in thy chamber of state. Thine ancient tower—a woman's dower—shall be a ruin and a beacon, until an ash sapling shall spring from its topmost stone. Then shall thy sorrows be ended, and the sunshine of royalty shall beam on thee once more. Thine honours shall be restored; the kiss of peace shall be given to thy Countess, though she seek it not, and the days of peace shall return to thee and thine. The line of Mar shall be broken; but not until its honours are doubled, and its doom is ended."

In support of this strange curse, it may be noted that the Earl of 1571 was raised to be Regent of Scotland, and guardian of James VI. As Regent, he commanded the destruction of Cambuskenneth Abbey, and took its stones to build himself a palace at Stirling, which never advanced farther than the façade, which has been popularly designated "Marr's Work."

In the year 1715, the Earl of Mar raised the banner of his Sovereign, the Chevalier James Stuart, son of James the Second, or Seventh. He was defeated at the battle of Sheriff-Muir, his title being forfeited, and his lands of Mar confiscated and sold by the Government to the Earl of Fife. His grandson and representative, John Francis, lived at Alloa Tower (which had been for some time the abode of James VI. as an infant) where, a fire breaking out in one of the rooms, Mrs. Erskine was burnt, and died, leaving, beside others, three children who were born blind, and who all lived to old age.

But this remarkable curse was to be further fulfilled, for at the commencement of the present century, upon the alarm of the French invasion, a troop of the cavalry and yeomen of the district took possession of the tower, and for a week fifty horses were stabled in its lordly hall; and in the year 1810, a party of visitors were surprised to find a weaver plying his loom in the grand old Chamber of State. Between the years 1815 and 1820, an ash sapling might be seen in the topmost stone, and many of those who "clasped it in their hands wondered if it really were the twig of destiny, and if they should ever live to see the prophecy fulfilled."

In the year 1822, George IV. visited Scotland and searched out the families who had suffered by supporting the Princes of the Stuart line. Foremost of them all was the Erskine of Mar, grandson of Mar who had raised the Chevalier's standard, and to him the King restored his earldom. John Francis, the grandson of the restored Earl, likewise came into favour, for when Queen Victoria accidentally met his Countess in a small room in Stirling Castle, and ascertained who she was, she detained her, and, after conversing with her, kissed her. Although the Countess had never been presented at St. James's, yet, in a marvellous way, "the kiss of peace was given to her, though she sought it not"; and then, after the curse had worked through 300 years, the "weird dreed out, and the doom of Mar was ended."[2]

Another instance which may be quoted relates to Sherborne Castle. According to the traditionary accounts handed down, it appears that Osmund, one of William the Conqueror's knights, who had been rewarded, among other possessions, with the castle and barony of Sherborne, in the decline of life determined to resign his temporal honours, and to devote himself exclusively to religion. In pursuance of this object, he obtained the Bishopric of Salisbury, to which he gave certain lands, but annexed to the gift the following conditional curse: "That whosoever should take those lands from the Bishopric, or diminish them in great or small, should be accursed, not only in this world, but in the world to come, unless in his lifetime he made restitution thereof." In a strange and wonderful manner this curse is said to have been more than once fulfilled. Upon Osmund's death, the castle and lands fell into the hands of the next bishop, Roger Niger, who was dispossessed of them by King Stephen, on whose death they were held by the Montagues, all of whom, it is affirmed, so long as they kept these lands, were subjected to grievous disasters, in so much that the male line became altogether extinct. About two hundred years from this time, the lands again reverted to the Church, but in the reign of Edward VI. the Castle of Sherborne was conveyed by the then Bishop of Sarum to the Duke of Somerset, who lost his head on Tower Hill. Sir Walter Raleigh, again, obtained the property from the crown, and it was to expiate this offence, it has been suggested, he ultimately lost his head. But in allusion to this reputed curse, Sir John Harrington gravely tells how it happened one day that Sir Walter riding post between Plymouth and the Court, "the castle being right in the way, he cast such an eye upon it as Ahab did upon Naboth's vineyard, and whilst talking of the commodiousness of the place, and of the great strength of the seat, and how easily it might be got from the Bishopric, suddenly over and over came his horse, and his very face—which was then thought a very good one—ploughed up the earth where he fell." Then again Prince Henry died shortly after he took possession, and Carr, Earl of Somerset, the next proprietor fell in disgrace. But the way the latter obtained Sherborne was far from creditable, for, having discovered a technical flaw in the deed in which Sir Walter Raleigh had settled the estate on his son, he solicited it of his royal master, and obtained it. It was in vain that Lady Raleigh on her knees appealed to James against this injustice, for he only answered, "I mun have the land, I mun have it for Carr." But Lady Raleigh was a woman of high spirit, and there on her knees, before King James, she prayed to God that He would punish those who had thus wrongfully exposed her, and her children, to ruin. She was, in fact, re-echoing the curse uttered centuries beforehand. And that prayer was not long unanswered, for Carr did not enjoy Sherborne for any length of time. Committed to the Tower for the murder of Sir Thomas Overbury, he was at last released and restricted to his house in the country, "where in constant companionship with the wife, for the guilty love of whom he had become the murderer of his friend, he passed the remainder of his life, loathing the partner of his crimes, and by her as cordially detested."

Spelman goes so far as to say that "all those families who took or had Church property presented to them, came, either in their own persons or those of their descendants, to sorrow and misfortune." One of the many strange occurrences relating to Sir Anthony Browne, standard-bearer to King Henry VIII., was communicated some years ago in connection with the famous Cowdray Castle, the principal seat of the Montagues. It is said that at the great festival given in the magnificent hall of the monks at Battle Abbey, on Sir Anthony Browne taking possession of his Sovereign's gift of that estate, a venerable monk stalked up the hall to the daïs, where Sir Anthony Browne sat, and, in prophetic language, denounced him and his posterity for usurping the possessions of the Church, predicting their destruction by fire and water—a fate which was eventually fulfilled.

One of the last viscounts was, in 1793, drowned when trying to pass the Falls of Schaffhausen on the Rhine, accompanied by Mr. Sedley Burdett, the elder brother of the distinguished Sir Francis. They had engaged an open boat to take them through the rapids; but it seems the authorities tried to prevent so dangerous an enterprise. In order, however, to carry out their project, they started two hours earlier than the time previously fixed—four o'clock in the morning—and successfully passed the first or upper fall. But, unhappily, the same good fortune failed them in their next descent, for "the boat was swamped and sunk in passing the lower fall, and was supposed to have been jammed in a cleft of the submerged rock, as neither boat nor adventurers ever appeared again. In the same week, the ancient seat of the family, Cowdray Castle, was destroyed by fire, and its venerable ruins are the significant monument at once of the fulfilment of the old monk's prophecy, and of the extinction of the race of the great and powerful noble."

It is further added that the last inheritor of the title—the immediate successor and cousin of the ill-fated young nobleman of Schaffhausen, Anthony Browne, the last Montague, who died at the opening of this century—left no male issue, and his estates devolved on his only daughter, who married Mr. Stephen Poyntz, a great Buckinghamshire landlord. Some years after their marriage Mr. Poyntz was desirous of obtaining a grant of the dormant title "Viscount Montague" in favour of the elder of his two sons, issue of this marriage; but his hopes were suddenly destroyed by the death of the two boys, who were drowned while bathing at Bognor, the "fatal water" thus becoming the means, in fulfilment of the monk's terrible denunciation on the family in his fearful curse.

In a similar manner the great Tichborne trial followed, it is said, upon the fulfilment, in a manner, of a prophecy, respecting that ancient family, made more than seven hundred years before. When the Lady Mabelle Tichborne, wife of the Sir Roger who flourished in the reign of Henry II., was lying on her death-bed, she besought her husband to grant her the means of leaving behind her a charitable bequest in the form of an annual dole of bread. To gratify her whim, he accordingly promised her the produce of as much land in the vicinity of the park as she could walk over while a certain brand was burning; for, as she had been bedridden for many years, he supposed that she would be able to go round only a small portion of the property. But when the venerable dame was carried out upon the ground, she seemed to regain her strength, and, greatly to the surprise of her husband, crawled round several rich and goodly acres, which, to this day, retain the name of "The Crawls." On being reconveyed to her chamber, Lady Mabelle summoned her family to her bedside and predicted its prosperity so long as the annual dole was observed, but she left her solemn curse on any of her descendants who should discontinue it, prophesying that when such should happen, the old house would fall, and the family name "become extinct from failure" of male issue. And she further added, that this would be foretold by a generation of seven sons being followed immediately after by a generation of seven daughters and no son.

The custom of the annual doles was observed for six hundred years on every 25th of March, until—owing to the complaints of the magistrates and local gentry that vagabonds, gipsies, and idlers of every description swarmed into the neighbourhood, under the pretence of receiving the dole—it was discontinued in the year 1796. Strangely enough, Sir Henry Tichborne, the baronet of that day, had issue seven sons, and his eldest son, who succeeded him, had seven daughters and no son. The prophecy was apparently completed by the change of name of the possessors of the estate to Doughty, in the person of Sir Edward Doughty, who had assumed the name under the will of a relative from whom he inherited certain property. Finally, it may be added, "the Claimant" appeared, and instituted one of the most costly lawsuits ever tried, in which the Tichborne estate was put to an expense of close upon one hundred thousand pounds!

But, occasionally, the effect of a family curse, through the misappropriation of property, has been more sweeping and speedy in its retribution, as in the case of Furvie or Forvie, which now forms part of the parish of Slains, Scotland—much, if not most of it, being covered with sand. The popular account of the downfall of this parish tells how, in times gone by, the proprietor to whom it belonged left three daughters as heirs of his fair lands; who were, however, most unjustly bereft of their property, and thrown homeless on the world. On quitting their home—their legal heritage—they uttered a terrible curse, which was quickly accomplished, and was considered an unmistakable sign of Divine displeasure at the wrong they had received. Before many days had elapsed, a storm of almost unparalleled violence—lasting nine days—burst over the district, and transformed the parish of Forvie into a desert of sand;—a calamity which is said to have befallen the district about the close of the 17th century. In this way, many local traditions account for the ruined and desolate condition of certain wild and uninhabited spots. Ettrick Hall, for instance, near the head of Ettrick Water, had such a history. On and around its site in former days there was a considerable village, and "as late as the Revolution, it contained no fewer than fifty-three fine houses." But about the year 1700, when the numbers in this little village were still very considerable, James Anderson, a member of the Tushielaw family, pulled down a number of small cottages, leaving many of the tenants—some of whom were aged and infirm—homeless. It was in vain that these poor people appealed to him for a little merciful consideration, for he refused to lend an ear to their complaints, and in a short time a splendid house was built on the property, known as Ettrick Hall. What was considered by the inhabitants far and wide as an act of cruel injustice incurred its own punishment, for a prophetic rhyme was about the same period made on it, by whom nobody could tell, and which, says James Hogg, writing in the year 1826, has been most wonderfully verified:

Ettrick Hall stands on yon plain,Right sore exposed to wind and rain;And on it the sun shines never at morn,Because it was built in the widow's corn;And its foundations can never be sure,Because it was built on the ruin of the poor.And or an age is come and gane,Or the trees o'er the chimly-taps grow green,We kinna wen where the house has been.

The curse that alighted on this fair mansion at length accomplished its destructive work, because nowadays there is not a vestige of it remaining, nor has there been for these many years; indeed, so complete was the collapse of this ill-fated house, that its site could only be identified by the avenue and lanes of trees; while many clay cottages, on the other hand, which were built previously, long remained intact. Equally fatal, also, was the curse uttered against the old persecuting family of Home of Cowdenknowes—a place in the immediate neighbourhood of St. Thomas's Castle.

Vengeance, vengeance! When and where?Upon the house of
Cowdenknowes, now and evermair!

   This anathema, awful as the cry of blood, is generally said to have been realised in the extinction of the family and the transference of their property to other hands. But some doubt, writes Mr. Robert Chambers,[3] seems to hang on the matter, "as the Earl of Home—a prosperous gentleman—is the lineal descendant of the Cowdenknowes branch of the family which acceded to the title in the reign of Charles I., though, it must be admitted, the estate has long been alienated."Love and marriage, again, have been associated with many imprecations, one of which dates as far back as the time of Edmund, King of the East Angles, in connection with his defeat and capture at Hoxne, in Suffolk, on the banks of the Waveney not far from Eye. The story, as told by Sir Francis Palgrave in his Anglo-Saxon History, is this: "Being hotly pursued by his foes, the King fled to Hoxne, and attempted to conceal himself by crouching beneath a bridge, now called Goldbridge. The glittering of his golden spurs discovered him to a newly-married couple, who were returning home by moonlight, and they betrayed him to the Danes. Edmund, as he was dragged from his hiding place, pronounced a malediction upon all who should afterwards pass this bridge on their way to be married. So much regard was paid to this tradition by the good folks of Hoxne that no bride or bridegroom would venture along the forbidden path."

   That inconstancy has not always escaped with impunity may be gathered from the following painful story, one which, if it had not been fully attested, would seem to belong to the domain of fiction rather than truth: On April 28, 1795, a naval court-martial, which had lasted for sixteen days, and created considerable excitement, was terminated. The officer tried was Captain Anthony James Pye Molloy, of H.M. Ship Cæsar and the charge brought against him was that, in the memorable battle of June 1, 1794, he did not bring his ship into action, and exert himself to the utmost of his power. The decision of the court was adverse to the Captain, but, "having found that on many previous occasions Captain Molloy's courage had been unimpeachable," he was sentenced to be dismissed his ship, instead of the penalty of death.

It is said that Captain Molloy had behaved dishonourably to a young lady to whom he was betrothed. The friends of the lady wished to bring an action for breach of promise against the Captain, but the lady declined doing so, only remarking that God would punish him. Some time afterwards the two accidentally met at Bath, when the lady confronted her inconstant lover by saying: "Capt. Molloy, you are a bad man. I wish you the greatest curse that can befall a British officer. When the day of battle comes, may your false heart fail you!"

Her words were fully realised, his subsequent conduct and irremediable disgrace forming the fulfilment of her wish.[4]

Another curse, which may be said to have a historic interest, has been popularly designated the "Midwife's Curse." It appears that Colonel Stephen Payne, who took a foremost part in striving to uphold the tottering fortunes of the Stuarts, had wooed and won a fair wife amid the battles of the Rebellion. The Duke of York promised to stand as godfather to the first child if it should prove a boy; but when a daughter was born, the Colonel in his mortification, it is said, "formally devoted, in succession, his hapless wife, his infant daughter, himself and his belongings, to the infernal deities."But the story goes that the midwife, Douce Vardon, was commissioned by the shade of Normandy's first duke to announce to her master that not only would his daughter die in infancy, but that neither he nor anyone descended from him would ever again be blessed with a daughter's love. Not many days afterwards the child died, "whose involuntary coming had been the cause of the Payne curse." Time passed on, and that "Heaven is merciful," writes Sir Bernard Burke,[5] Stephen Payne experienced in his own person, for his wife subsequently presented him with a son, who was sponsored by the Duke of York by proxy. "But six generations of the descendants of Colonel Stephen Payne," it is added, "have come and gone since the utterance of the midwife's curse, but they never yet have had a daughter born to them." Such is the immutability of the decrees of Fate.

FOOTNOTES:

[1] Harland's "Lancashire Legends" (1882), 4, 5.

[2] See Sir J. Bernard Burke's "Family Romance," 1853.

[3] "Popular Rhymes of Scotland" (1870), 217-18.

[4] See "Book of Days," I., 559.

[5] "The Rise of Great Families," 191-202.

CHAPTER II.
THE SCREAMING SKULL.

"Look on its broken arch, its ruined wall,
Its chambers desolate, its portals foul;
Yes, this was once Ambition's airy hall—
The dome of thought, the palace of the soul."

BYRON.

There are told of certain houses, in different parts of the country, many weird skull stories, the popular idea being that if any profane hand should be bold enough to remove, or in any way tamper with, such gruesome relics of the dead, misfortune will inevitably overtake the family. Hence, for years past, there have been carefully preserved in some of our country homes numerous skulls, all kinds of romantic traditions accounting for their present isolated and unburied condition.

An old farmstead known as Bettiscombe, near Bridport, Dorsetshire, has long been famous for its so-called "screaming skull," generally supposed to be that of a negro servant who declared before his death that his spirit would not rest until his body was buried in his native land. But, contrary to his dying wish, he was interred in the churchyard of Bettiscombe, and hence the trouble which this skull has ever since occasioned. In the August of 1883, Dr. Richard Garnett, his daughter, and a friend, while staying in the neighbourhood determined to pay this eccentric skull a visit, the result of which is thus amusingly told by Miss Garnett:

"One fine afternoon a party of three adventurous spirits started off, hoping to discover the skull and investigate its history. This much we knew, that the skull would only scream when it was buried, and so we hoped to get leave to inter it in the churchyard. The village of Bettiscombe was at length reached, and we found our way to the old farmhouse, which stood at the end of the village by itself. It had evidently been a manor house, and a very handsome one, too. We were admitted into a fine paved hall, and attempted to break the ice by asking for milk. We then endeavoured to draw the good woman of the house into conversation by admiring the place, and asking in a guarded manner respecting the famous skull. On this subject she was most reserved. She had only lately had the farmhouse, and had been obliged to take possession of the skull also; but she did not wish us to suppose that she knew much about it; it was a veritable 'skeleton in the closet' to her. After exercising great diplomacy, we persuaded her to allow us a sight of it. We tramped up the fine old staircase till we reached the top of the house, when, opening a cupboard door, she showed us a steep, winding staircase, leading to the roof, and from one of the steps the skull sat grinning at us. We took it in our hands and examined it carefully; it was very old and weather-beaten, and certainly human. The lower jaw was missing, the forehead very low and badly proportioned. One of our party, who was a medical student, examined it long and gravely, and then, after first telling the good woman that he was a doctor, pronounced it to be, in his opinion, the skull of a negro. After this oracular utterance, she resolved to make a clean breast of all she knew, which, however, did not amount to much. The skull, we were informed, was that of a negro servant, who had lived in the service of a Roman Catholic priest. Some difference arose between them; but whether the priest murdered the servant, in order to conceal some crimes known to the negro, or whether the negro, in a fit of passion, killed his master, did not clearly appear.

However, the negro had declared before his death that his spirit would not rest unless his body was taken to his native land and buried there. This was not done, he being buried in the churchyard of Bettiscombe. Then the haunting began; fearful screams proceeded from the grave, the doors and windows of the house rattled and creaked, strange sounds were heard all over the house; in short, there was no rest for the inmates until the body was dug up. At different periods attempts were made to bury the body, but similar disturbances always recurred. In process of time the skeleton disappeared, 'all save the skull,' and its reputation as 'the screaming skull' remains unimpaired."

In a farm-house in Sussex are preserved two skulls from Hastings Priory, about which many gruesome stories are current in the neighbourhood. One of these skulls, it appears, has been in the house many years; the other was placed there by a former tenant of the farm. It is the prevalent impression in the locality, that, if by any chance the former skull were to be removed, the cattle in the farm would die, and unearthly sounds be heard in and about the house at night time. According to a local tradition, the skull belonged to a man who murdered the owner of the house, and marks of blood are pointed out on the floor of the adjoining room, where the murder is said to have been committed, and which no washing will remove. But, on more than one occasion, the skull has been taken away without any ill-effects, and, one year, was placed by a profane hand in a branch of a neighbouring tree, where it remained a whole summer, during which time a bird's nest was constructed within it, and a young brood successfully reared.

And yet the old superstition still survives, and the prejudice against tampering with this peculiar skull has in no way diminished.[6]

There are the remains of a skull, in three parts, at Tunstead, a farmhouse about a mile and a half from Chapel-en-le-Frith, which, although popularly known by the male cognomen "Dickie," has always been said to be that of a woman. How long it has been located in its present home is not known, but tradition tells how one of two co-heiresses residing here was murdered, who solemnly affirmed that her bones should remain in the place for ever. In days past, this skull has been guilty of all sorts of eccentric pranks, many of which are still told by the credulous peasantry with respectful awe. It is added,[7] also, that if "Dickie" should accidentally be removed, everything in the farm will go wrong. The cows will be dry and barren, the sheep have the rot, and horses fall down, breaking their knees and otherwise injuring themselves. The story goes, too, that when the London and North-Western Railway to Manchester was being made, the foundations of a bridge gave way in the yielding sands and bog, and, after several attempts to build the bridge had failed, it was found necessary to divert the highway, and pass it under the railway on higher ground. These engineering failures were attributed to the malevolent influence of "Dickie," but as soon as the road was diverted it was bridged successfully, because no longer in Dickie's territory.

A similar superstition attaches to a skull kept in a farmhouse at Chilton Cantelo, in Somersetshire. From the date on the tombstone of the former owner of the skull—1670—it has been conjectured that he came to the retired village, in which he was buried, after taking an active part, on the Republican side, in the Civil War; and that seeing the way in which the bodies of some of them who had acted with him were treated after the Restoration, he wished to provide against this in his own case. But, whatever the previous history of this curious skull, it has at times caused a good deal of trouble, resenting any proposal to consign it to the earth, for buried it will not be, no matter how many attempts are made to do so. Strange to say, most of this class of skulls behave in the same extraordinary fashion. At a short distance from Turton Tower—one of the most interesting structures in the neighbourhood of Bolton—is a farmhouse locally designated Timberbottom, or the Skull House, so called from the circumstance that two skulls are or were kept there, one of which was much decayed, whereas the other appeared to have been cut through by a blow from some sharp instrument. These skulls, it is said, have been buried many times in the graveyard at Bradshaw Chapel, but they have always had to be exhumed, and brought back to the farm-house. On one occasion, they were thrown into the adjacent river, but to no purpose; for they had to be fished up and restored to their old quarters before the ghosts of their owners could once more rest in peace.

A popular cause assigned for this strange behaviour on the part of certain skulls is that their owners met with a violent death, and that the avenging spirit in this manner annoys the living, reminding us of Macbeth's words:

"Blood hath been shed ere now, i' the olden time,Ere human statute purg'd the gentle weal;Ay, and since too, murders have been performedToo terrible for the ear; the times have beenThat, when the brains were out, the man would dieAnd there an end; but now they rise again,With twenty mortal murders on their crowns,And push us from our stools. This is more strangeThan such a murder is."

Hence, a romantic and tragic story is told of two skulls which have long haunted an old house near Ambleside. It appears that a small piece of ground, known as Calgrath, was owned by a humble farmer, named Kraster Cook, and his wife Dorothy. But their little inheritance was coveted by a wealthy magistrate, Myles Phillipson, who, unable to induce them to part with it, swore "he'd have that ground, be they 'live or dead." As time wore on, however, he appeared more gracious to Kraster and Dorothy, and actually invited them to a great Christmas banquet given to the neighbours. It was a dear feast for them, for Myles Phillipson pretended they had stolen a silver cup, and, sure enough, it was found in Kraster's house—a "plant," of course. Such an offence was then capital, and, as Phillipson was the magistrate, Kraster and Dorothy were sentenced to death. Thereupon, Dorothy arose in the court-room and addressed Phillipson in words that rang through the building and impressed all for their awful earnestness:

"Guard thyself, Myles Phillipson! Thou thinkest thou hast managed grandly, but that tiny lump of land is the dearest a Phillipson has ever bought or stolen, for you will never prosper, neither your breed. Whatever scheme you undertake will wither in your hand; the side you take will always lose; the time shall come when no Phillipson shall own an inch of land; and while Calgarth walls shall stand we'll haunt it night and day. Never will ye be rid of us!"

Henceforth, the Phillipsons had for their guests two skulls. They were found at Christmas at the head of a staircase. They were buried in a distant region, but they turned up in the old house again. Again and again were the two skulls burned; they were brazed to dust and cast to the winds, and for several years they were cast in the lake, but the Phillipsons could never get rid of them. In the meantime, Dorothy's weird went steadily on to its fulfilment, until the family sank into poverty, and at length disappeared.[8]

As a more rational explanation of the matter, it is told by some local historians "that there formerly lived in the house a famous doctress, who had two skeletons by her for the usual purposes of her profession, and these skulls, happening to meet with better preservation than the rest of the bones, they were accidentally honoured" with this singular tradition.[9]

Wardley Hall, Lancashire, has its skull, which is supposed to be the witness of some tragedy committed in the past, and to have belonged to Roger Downes, the last male representative of his family, and who was one of the most abandoned courtiers of Charles II. Roby, in one of his "Traditions," entitled "The Skull House," has represented him as rushing forth "hot from the stews," drawing his sword as he staggered along, and swearing that he would kill the first man he met. Terrible to say, that fearful oath was fulfilled, for his victim was a poor tailor, whom he ran through with his weapon and killed on the spot. He was apprehended for the crime, but his interest at Court quickly procured him a free pardon, and he soon continued his reckless course. But one evening, as his sister and cousin Eleanor were chatting together at Wardley, the carrier from Manchester brought a wooden box, "which had come all the way from London by Antony's waggon." Suspecting that there was something mysterious connected with this package, for the direction was "a quaint, crabbed hand," she opened it in secret, when, to her amazement and horror, this writing attracted her notice:

"Thy brother has at length paid the forfeit of his crimes. The wages of sin is death! And his head is before thee. Heaven hath avenged the innocent blood he hath shed. Last night, in the lusty vigour of a drunken debauch, passing over London Bridge, he encounters another brawl, wherein, having run at the watchmen with his rapier, one blow of the bill which they carried severed thy brother's head from his trunk. The latter was cast over the parapet into the river. The head only remained, which an eye witness, if not a friend, hath sent to thee!" His sister tried at first to keep the story of her brother's death a secret, and hid with all speed this ghastly memorial for ever, as she hoped, from the gaze and knowledge of the world. It was her desire to conceal this foul stain upon the family name, but "the grave gives back its dead. The charnel gapes. The ghastly head hath burst its cold tabernacle, and risen from the dust." No human power could drive it away. It hath "been torn in pieces, burnt, and otherwise destroyed, but even on the subsequent day it is seen filling its wonted place. Yet it was always observed that sore vengeance lighted on its persecutors. One who hacked it in pieces was seized with such horrible torments in his limbs that it seemed as though he might be undergoing the same process. Sometimes, if only displaced, a fearful storm would arise, so loud and terrible that the very elements themselves seemed to become the ministers of its wrath." Nor will this eccentric piece of mortality allow the little aperture in which it rests to be walled up, for it remains there still, whitened and bleached by the weather, "looking forth from those rayless sockets upon the scenes which, when living, they had once beheld." Towards the close of the last century, Thomas Barritt, the Manchester antiquary, visited this skull—"this surprising piece of household furniture," as he calls it, and adds that "one of us who was last in company with it, removed it from its place into a dark part of the room, and there left it, and returned home." But on the following night a violent storm arose in the neighbourhood, causing an immense deal of damage—trees being blown down and roofs unthatched—and the cause, as it was supposed, being ascertained, the skull was replaced, when these terrific disturbances ceased. And yet, as Thomas Barritt sensibly remarks, "All this might have happened had the skull never been removed; but withal it keeps alive the credibility of the tradition." Formerly two keys were provided for this "place of a skull," one being kept by the tenant of the Hall, and the other by the Countess of Ellesmere, the owner of the property. The Countess occasionally accompanied visitors from the neighbouring Worsley Hall, and herself unlocked the door, and revealed to her friends the grinning skull of Wardley Hall.[10]

SHE OPENED IT IN SECRET

Another romantic story is associated with Burton Agnes Hall, between Bridlington and Driffield, Yorkshire, which is haunted by the spirit of a lady a former co-heiress of the estate—who is popularly known as "Awd Nance." The skull of this lady is carefully preserved in the Hall, and so long as it is left undisturbed all goes well, but whenever any attempt is made to remove it, the most unearthly noises are heard in the house, and last until it is restored. According to a local tradition, many years ago the three co-heiresses of the estate of Burton Agnes were possessed of considerable wealth, and finding the ancient mansion, in which they resided, not in harmony with their ideas of what a home should be suited to their position, determined to erect a house in such a style as should eclipse all others in the neighbourhood. The most prominent organiser of the scheme was the younger sister, Anne, who could talk or think of nothing but the magnificent home about to be built, which in due time, it is said, "emerged from the hands of artists and workmen, like a palace erected by the genii of the Arabian Nights, a palace encrusted throughout on walls, roof, and furniture with the most exquisite carvings and sculptures of the most skilled masters of the age, and radiant with the most glowing tints of the pencil of Peter Paul."

But soon after its completion and occupation by its three co-heiresses, Anne, the enthusiast, paid an afternoon visit to the St. Quentins, at Harpham. On starting to return home about nightfall with her dog, she had gone no great distance when she was confronted by two ruffianly-looking beggars, who asked alms. She readily gave them a few coins, and in doing so the glitter of her finger-ring accidentally attracted their notice, which they at once demanded should be given up to them. This she refused to do, as it had been her mother's ring, and was one which she valued above all price.

"Mother or no mother," gruffly replied one of the rogues, "we mean to have it, and if you do not part with it freely, we must take it," whereupon he seized her hand and attempted to drag off the ring.

Frightened at this act of violence, Anne screamed for help, at which the other ruffian, exclaiming, "Stop that noise!" struck her a blow, and she fell senseless to the earth. But her screams had attracted attention, and the approach of some villagers caused the villains to make a hasty retreat, without being able to get the ring from her finger. In a dying condition, as it was supposed, Anne was carried back to Harpham Hall, where, under the care of Lady St. Quentin, she made sufficient recovery to be removed the following day to her own home. The brutal treatment she had received from the highwaymen, however, had done its fatal work, and after a few days, during which she was alternately sensible and delirious, she succumbed to the effects. Her one thought previous to death was her devotion to her home, which had latterly been the ruling passion of her life; and bidding her sisters farewell, she addressed them thus:—

"Sisters, never shall I sleep peacefully in my grave in the churchyard unless I, or a part of me at least, remain here in our beautiful home as long as it lasts. Promise me this, dear sisters, that when I am dead my head shall be taken from my body and preserved within these walls. Here let it for ever remain, and on no account be removed. And understand and make it known to those who in future shall become possessors of the house, that if they disobey this my last injunction, my spirit shall, if so able and so permitted, make such a disturbance within its walls as to render it uninhabitable for others so long as my head is divorced from its home."

Her sisters promised to accede to her dying request, but failed to do so, and her body was laid entire under the pavement of the church. Within a few days Burton Agnes Hall was disturbed by the most alarming noises, and no servant could be induced to remain in the house. In this dilemma, the two sisters remembered that they had not carried out Anne's last wish, and, at the suggestion of the clergyman, the coffin was opened, when a strange sight was seen. The "body lay without any marks of corruption or decay; but the head was disengaged from the trunk, and appeared to be rapidly assuming the semblance of a fleshless skull." This was reported to the two sisters, and on the vicar's advice the skull of Anne was taken to Burton Agnes Hall, where, so long as it remained undisturbed, no ghostly noises were heard. It may be added that numerous attempts have from time to time been made to rid the hall of this skull, but without success.

Many other similar skulls are still existing in various places, and, in addition to their antiquarian interest, have attracted the sightseer, connected as they mostly are with tales of legendary romance. An amusing anecdote of a skull is told by the late Mr. Wirt Sikes.[11] It seems that on a certain day some men were drinking at an inn when one of them, to show his courage and want of superstition, affirmed that he was "afraid of no ghosts," and dared to go to the church and fetch a skull. This he did, and after an hour or so of merrymaking over the skull, he carried it back to where he had found it; but, as he was leaving the church, "suddenly a tremendous blast like a whirlwind seized him, and so mauled him that he ever after maintained that nothing should induce him to do such a thing again." The man was still more convinced that the ghost of the original owner of the skull had been after him, when his wife informed him that the cane which hung in his room had been beating against the wall in a dreadful manner.

Byron had his skull romance at Newstead, but in this case the skull was more orderly, and not given to those unpleasant pranks of which other skulls have seemingly been guilty. Whilst living at Newstead, a skull was one day found of large dimensions and peculiar whiteness. Concluding that it belonged to some friar who had been domesticated at Newstead—prior to the confiscation of the monasteries by Henry VIII.—Byron determined to convert it into a drinking vessel, and for this purpose dispatched it to London, where it was elegantly mounted. On its return to Newstead, he instituted a new order at the Abbey, constituting himself grand master, or abbot, of the skull. The members, twelve in number, were provided with black gowns—that of Byron, as head of the fraternity, being distinguished from the rest. A chapter was held at certain times, when the skull drinking goblet was filled with claret, and handed about amongst the gods of this consistory, whilst many a grim joke was cracked at the expense of this relic of the dead. The following lines were inscribed upon it by Byron:

Start not, nor deem my spirit fled;In me behold the only skullFrom which, unlike a living head,Whatever flows is never dull.

I lived, I loved, I quaff'd, like thee;I died: let earth my bones resign.Fill up, thou canst not injure me;The worm hath fouler lips than mine.

Where once my wit, perchance, hath shone,In aid of others, let me shine,And when, alas! our brains are gone,What nobler substitute than wine.

Quaff while thou canst. Another race,When thou and thine, like me, are sped,May rescue thee from earth's embrace,And rhyme and revel with the dead.

Why not? since through life's little dayOur heads such sad effects produce;Redeem'd from worms and wasting clay,This chance is theirs, to be of use.

    The skull, it is said, is buried beneath the floor of the chapel at Newstead Abbey.

FOOTNOTES:

[6] Sussex Archæological Collections xiii. 162-3.

[7] See Notes and Queries, 4th S., XI. 64.

[8] Told by Mr. Moncure Conway in Harper's Magazine.

[9] "Tales and Legends of the English Lakes," 96-7.

[10] "Harland's Lancashire Legends," 1882, 65-70.

[11] "British Goblins," 1880, p. 146.

CHAPTER III.
ECCENTRIC VOWS.

> No man takes or keeps a vow,
> But just as he sees others do;
> Nor are they 'bliged to be so brittle
> As not to yield and bow a little:
> For as best tempered blades are found
> Before they break, to bend quite round,
> So truest oaths are still more tough,
> And, tho' they bow, are breaking-proof.
>
> BUTLER'S "Hudibras," Ep. to his Lady, 75.

Some two hundred and fifty years ago, the prevailing colour in all dresses was that shade of brown known as the "couleur Isabelle," and this was its origin:—A short time after the siege of Ostend commenced, at the beginning of the seventeenth century, Isabella Eugenia, Gouvernante of the Netherlands, incensed at the obstinate bravery of the defenders, is reported to have made a vow that she would not change her chemise till the town surrendered. It was a marvellously inconvenient vow, for the siege, according to the precise historians thereof, lasted three years, three months, three weeks, three days, and three hours; and her highness's garment had wonderfully changed its colour before twelve months of the time had expired. But the ladies and gentlemen of the Court, in no way dismayed, resolved to keep their mistress in countenance, and, after a struggle between their loyalty and their cleanliness, they hit upon the compromising expedient of wearing dresses of the presumed colour, finally attained by the garment which clung to the Imperial Archduchess by force of religious obstinacy. But, foolish and eccentric as was the conduct of Isabella Eugenia, there have been persons gifted, like herself, with sufficient mental power and strength of character to keep the vows they have sworn.

Thus, at a tournament held on the 17th November, 1559—the first anniversary of Queen Elizabeth's accession—Sir Henry Lee, of Quarendon, made a vow that every year on the return of that auspicious day, he would present himself in the tilt yard, in honour of the Queen, to maintain her beauty, worth, and dignity, against all comers, unless prevented by infirmity, accident, or age. Elizabeth accepted Sir Henry as her knight and champion;

and the nobility and gentry of the Court formed themselves into an Honourable Society of Knights Tilters, which held a grand tourney every 17th November. But in the year 1590, Sir Henry, on account of age, resigned his office, having previously, by Her Majesty's permission, appointed the famous Earl of Cumberland as his successor. On this occasion, the royal choir sang the following verses as Sir Henry Lee's farewell to the Court:

My golden locks time hath to silver turned,O Time, too swift, and swiftness never ceasing!My youth 'gainst age, and age at youth both spurned,But spurned in vain—youth waned by increasing;Beauty, and strength, and youth, flowers fading been;Duty, faith, love, are roots and evergreen.

My helmet now shall make a hive for bees,And lover's songs shall turn to holy psalms;A man-at arms must now sit on his knees,And feed on prayers that are old age's alms.And so from Court to cottage I depart,My Saint is sure of mine unspotted heart.

And when I sadly sit in homely cell,I'll teach my saints this carol for a song:Blest be the hearts that wish my sovereign well!Cursed be the souls that think to do her wrong!Goddess! vouchsafe this aged man his rightTo be your beadsman now, that was your knight.

But not long after Sir Henry Lee had resigned his office of especial champion of the beauty of the sovereign, he fell in love with the new maid of honour—the fair Mrs. Anne Vavasour—who, though in the morning flower of her charms, and esteemed the loveliest girl in the whole court, drove a whole bevy of youthful lovers to despair by accepting this ancient relic of the age of chivalry.[12]

Queen Isabella vowed to make a pilgrimage to Barcelona, and return thanks at the tomb of that City's patron Saint, if the Infanta Eulalie recovered from an apparently mortal illness, and Queen Joan of Naples honoured the knight Galeazzo of Mantua by opening the ball with him at a grand feast at her castle of Gaita. At the conclusion of the dance, Galeazzo, kneeling down before his royal partner, vowed, as an acknowledgment of the honour he had received, to visit every country where feats of arms were performed, and not to rest until he had subdued two valiant knights, and presented them as prisoners to the queen, to be disposed of at her royal pleasure. After an absence of twelve months, Galeazzo, true to his vow, appeared at Naples, and laid his two prisoners at the feet of Queen Joan, but who, it is said, displayed commendable wisdom on the occasion, and "declined her right to impose rigorous conditions on her captives, and gave them liberty without ransom."

Such cases, it is true, have been somewhat rare, for made oftentimes on the impulse of the moment, "unheedful vows," as Shakespeare says, "may heedfully be broken." But, scarce as the records of unbroken vows may be, they are deserving of a permanent record, more especially as the direction of their eccentricity is, for the most part, in itself curious and uncommon. Love, for instance, has been responsible for many strange and curious vows in the past, and some years ago it was stated that the original of Charles Dickens's Miss Havisham was living in the flesh not far from Ventnor in the person of an old maiden lady, who, because of the maternal objection to some love affair in her early life, made and kept a vow that she would retire to her bed, and there spend the remainder of her days. It was a stern vow but she kept her word, "and the years have come and gone, and the house has never been swept or garnished, the garden is an overgrown tangle, and the eccentric lady has spent twenty years between the sheets." But whether this piece of romance is to be accepted or not, love has been the cause of many foolish acts, and many a disappointed damsel, has acted in no less eccentric a fashion than Miss Havisham, who was so completely overcome by the failure of Compeyson to appear on the wedding morning that she became fossilised, and gave orders that everything was to be kept unchanged, but to remain as it had been on that hapless day. Henceforth she was always attired in her bridal dress with lace veil from head to foot, white shoes, bridal flowers in her white hair, and jewels on her hands and neck. Years went on, the wedding breakfast remained set on the table, while the poor half demented lady flitted from one room to another like a restless ghost; and the case is recorded of another lady whose lover was arrested for forgery on the day before their marriage was to have taken place. Her vow took the form of keeping to her room, sitting winter and summer alike at her casement and waiting for him who was turning the treadmill, and who was never to come again.

On the other hand, vows have been made, but persons have contrived to rid themselves of the inconveniences without breaking them, reminding us of Benedick, who finding the charms of his "Dear Lady Disdain" too much for his celibate resolves, gets out of his difficulty by declaring that "When I said I would die a bachelor, I did not think I should live till I were married." Equally ludicrous, also, is the story told of a certain man, who, greatly terrified in a storm, vowed he would eat no haberdine, but, just as the danger was over, he qualified his promise with "Not without mustard, O Lord." And Voltaire, in one of his romances, represents a disconsolate widow vowing that she will never marry again, "so long as the river flows by the side of the hill." But a few months afterwards the widow recovers from her grief, and, contemplating matrimony, takes counsel with a clever engineer. He sets to work, the river is deviated from its course, and, in a short time, it no longer flows by the side of the hill. The lady, released from her vow, does not allow many days to elapse before she exchanges her weeds for a bridal veil. However far fetched this little romance may be, a veritable instance of thus keeping the letter of the vow and neglecting the spirit, was recorded not so very long ago: A Salopian parish clerk seeing a woman crossing the churchyard with a bundle and a watering can, followed her, curious to know what intentions might be, and discovered that she was a widow of a few months' standing. Inquiring what she was going to do with the watering pot, she informed him that she had been obtaining some grass seed to sow on her husband's grave, and had brought a little water to make it spring up quickly. The clerk told her there was no occasion to trouble, the grave would be green in good time. "Ah! that may be," she replied, "but my poor husband made me take a vow not to marry again until the grass had grown over his grave, and, having a good offer, I do not wish to break my vow, or keep as I am longer than I can help."

But vows have not always been broken with impunity. Janet Dalrymple, daughter of the first Lord Stair, secretly engaged herself to Lord Rutherford, who was not acceptable to her parents, either on account of his political principles, or his want of fortune. The young couple broke a piece of gold together, and pledged their troth in the most solemn manner, the young lady, it is said, imprecating dreadful evils on herself should she break her plighted faith. But shortly afterwards another suitor sought the hand of Janet Dalrymple, and, when she showed a cold indifference to his overtures, her mother, Lady Stair, insisted upon her consenting to marry the new suitor, David Dunbar, son and heir of David Dunbar of Baldoon, in Wigtonshire. It was in vain that Janet Dalrymple confessed her secret engagement, for Lady Stair treated this objection as a mere trifle.

Lord Rutherford, apprised of what had happened, interfered by letter, and insisted on the right he had acquired by his troth plighted with Janet Dalrymple. But Lady Stair answered in reply that "her daughter, sensible of her undutiful behaviour in entering into a contract unsanctioned by her parents, had retracted her unlawful vow, and now refused to fulfil her engagement with him." Lord Rutherford wrote again to Lady Stair, and briefly informed her that "he declined positively to receive such an answer from anyone but Janet Dalrymple," and, accordingly, an interview was arranged between them, at which Lady Stair took good care to be present, with pertinacity insisting on the Levitical law, which declares that a woman shall be free of a vow which her parents dissent from.

While Lady Stair insisted on her right to break the engagement, Lord Rutherford in vain entreated Janet Dalrymple to declare her feelings; but she remained "mute, pale, and motionless as a statue," and it was only at her mother's command, sternly uttered, she summoned strength enough to restore the broken piece of gold—the emblem of her troth. At this unexpected act Lord Rutherford burst into a tremendous passion, took leave of Lady Stair with maledictions, and, as he left the room, gave one angry glance at Janet Dalrymple, remarking, "For you, madam, you will be a world's wonder"—a phrase denoting some remarkable degree of calamity.

In due time, the marriage between Janet Dalrymple and David Dunbar of Baldoon, took place, the bride showing no repugnance, but being absolutely impassive in everything Lady Stair commanded or advised, always maintaining the same sad, silent, and resigned look.

The bridal feast was followed by dancing, and the bride and bridegroom retired as usual, when suddenly the most wild and piercing cries were heard from the nuptial chamber, which at length became so hideous that a general rush was made to learn the cause. On opening the door a ghastly scene presented itself, for the bridegroom was discovered lying on the floor, dreadfully wounded, and streaming with blood. The bride was seen sitting in the corner of the large chimney, dabbled in gore—grinning—in short, absolutely insane, and the only words she uttered were; "Take up your bonny bridegroom." She survived this tragic event little over a fortnight, having been married on the 24th August, and dying on the 12th September.

The unfortunate bridegroom recovered from his wounds, but, strange to say, he never permitted anyone to ask him respecting the manner in which he had received them; but he did not long survive this dreadful catastrophe, meeting with a fatal injury by a fall from a horse as he was one day riding between Leith and Holyrood House. As might be expected, various reports went abroad respecting this mysterious affair, most of them being inaccurate.[13] But the story has gained a lasting notoriety from Sir Walter Scott having founded his "Bride of Lammermoor" upon it; who, in his introductory notes to that novel, has given some curious facts concerning this tragic occurrence, quoting an elegy of Andrew Symson, which takes the form of a dialogue between a passenger and a domestic servant. The first recollecting that he had passed Lord Stair's house lately, and seen all around enlivened by mirth and festivity, is desirous of knowing what has changed so gay a scene into mourning, whereupon the servant replies:—

"Sir, 'tis truth you've told,We did enjoy great mirth; but now, ah me!Our joyful song's turned to an elegie.A virtuous lady, not long since a bride,Was to a hopeful plant by marriage tied,And brought home hither. We did all rejoiceEven for her sake. But presently her voiceWas turned to mourning for that little timeThat she'd enjoy: she waned in her prime,For Atropos, with her impartial knife,Soon cut her thread, and therewithal her life;And for the time, we may it well rememberIt being in unfortunate September;Where we must leave her till the resurrection,'Tis then the Saints enjoy their full perfection."

Many a vow too rashly made has been followed by an equally tragic result, instances of which are to be met with in the legendary lore of our county families. A somewhat curious legend is connected with a monument in the church of Stoke d'Abernon, Surrey. The story goes that two young brothers of the family of Vincent, the elder of whom had just come into his estate, were out shooting on Fairmile Common, about two miles from the village. They had put up several birds, but had not been able to get a single shot, when the elder swore with an oath that he would fire at whatever they next met with. They had not gone far before a neighbouring miller passed them, whereupon the younger brother reminded the elder of his oath, who immediately fired at the miller, and killed him on the spot. Through the influence of his family, backed by large sums of money, no effective steps were taken to apprehend young Vincent, but, after leading a life of complete seclusion for some years, death finally put an end to the insupportable anguish of his mind.

A pretty romance is told of Furness Abbey, locally known as "The Abbey Vows." Many years ago, Matilda, the pretty and much-admired daughter of a squire residing near Stainton, had been wooed and won by James, a neighbouring farmer's son. But as Matilda was the only child, her father fondly imagined that her rare beauty and fortune combined would procure her a good match, little thinking that her heart was already given to one whose position he would never recognise. It so happened, however, that the young people, through force of circumstances, were separated, neither seeing nor hearing of each other for some years.

At last, by chance, they were thrown together, when the active service in which James was employed had given his fine manly form an appearance which was at once imposing and captivating. Matilda, too, was improved in every eye, and never had James seen so lovely a maid as his former playmate. Their youthful hearts were disengaged, and they soon resolved to render their attachment as binding and as permanent as it was pure and undivided. The period had arrived, also, when James must again go to sea, and leave Matilda to have her fidelity tried by other suitors. Both, therefore, were willing to bind themselves by some solemn pledge to live but for each other. For this purpose they repaired, on the evening before James's departure, to the ruins of Furness Abbey. It was a fine autumnal evening; the sun had set in the greatest beauty, and the moon was hastening up the eastern sky; and in the roofless choir they knelt, near where the altar formerly stood, and repeated, in the presence of Heaven, their vows of deathless love.

They parted. But the fate of the betrothed lovers was a melancholy one. James returned to his ship for foreign service, and was killed by the first broadside of a French privateer, with which the captain had injudiciously ventured to engage. As for Matilda, she regularly went to the abbey to visit the spot where she had knelt with her lover; and there, it is said, "she would stand for hours, with clasped hands, gazing on that heaven which alone had been witness to their mutual vows."

Another momentous vow, but one of a terribly tragic nature, relates to Samlesbury Hall, which stands about midway between Preston and Blackburn, and has long been famous for its apparition of "The Lady in White." The story generally told is that one of the daughters of Sir John Southworth, a former owner, formed an attachment with the heir of a neighbouring house, and nothing was wanting to complete their happiness except the consent of the lady's father. Sir John was accordingly consulted by the youthful couple, but the tale of their love for each other only increased his rage, and he dismissed them with the most bitter denunciations.

"No daughter of his should ever be united to the son of a family which had deserted its ancestral faith," he solemnly vowed, and to intensify his disapproval of the whole affair, he forbade the young man his presence for ever. Difficulty, however, only served to increase the ardour of the lovers, and, after many secret interviews among the wooded slopes of the Ribble, an elopement was arranged, in the hope that time would eventually bring her father's forgiveness. But the day and place were unfortunately overheard by the lady's brother, who had hidden himself in a thicket close by, determined, if possible, to prevent what he considered to be his sister's disgrace. On the evening agreed upon both parties met at the appointed hour, and, as the young knight moved away with his betrothed, her brother rushed from his hiding-place, and, in pursuance of a vow he had made, slew him. After this tragic occurrence, Lady Dorothy was sent abroad to a convent, where she was kept under strict surveillance; but her mind at last gave way—the name of her murdered sweetheart was ever on her lips—and she died a raving maniac. It is said that on certain clear, still evenings, a lady in white can be seen passing along the gallery and the corridors, and then from the hall into the grounds, where she meets a handsome knight, who receives her on his bended knees, and he then accompanies her along the walks. On arriving at a certain spot, in all probability the lover's grave, both the phantoms stand still, and as they seem to utter soft wailings of despair, they embrace each other, and then their forms rise slowly from the earth and melt away into the clear blue of the surrounding sky.[14]

A strange and romantic story is told of Blenkinsopp Castle, which, too, has long been haunted by a "white lady." It seems that its owner, Bryan de Blenkinsopp, despite many good qualities, had an inordinate love of wealth which ultimately wrecked his fortune. At the marriage feast of a brother warrior with a lady of high rank and fortune, the health was drunk of Bryan de Blenkinsopp and his "lady love." But to the surprise of all present Bryan made a vow that "never shall that be until I meet with a lady possessed of a chest of gold heavier than ten of my strongest men can carry into my Castle." Soon afterwards he went abroad, and after an absence of twelve years returned, not only with a wife, but possessed of a box of gold that took three of the strongest men to convey it to the Castle. A grand banquet was given in honour of his return, and, after several days feasting and rejoicing, vague rumours were spread of dissensions between the lord and his lady. One day the young husband disappeared, and never returned to Blenkinsopp, nothing more being heard of him. But the traditionary account of this mystery asserts that his young wife, filled with remorse at her undutiful conduct towards him, cannot rest in her grave, but must wander about the old castle, and mourn over the chest of gold—the cursed cause of all their misery—of which it is supposed she, with the assistance of others, had deprived her husband. It is generally admitted that the cause of Bryan de Blenkinsopp's future unhappiness was the rash vow he uttered at that fatal banquet.

Associated with this curious romance there are current in the neighbourhood many tales of a more or less legendary character, but there has long been a firm belief that treasure lies buried beneath the crumbling ruins. According to one story given in Richardson's "Table Book of Traditions" some years ago, two of the more habitable apartments of Blenkinsopp Castle were utilized by a labourer of the estate and his family. But one night, the parents were aroused by screams from the adjoining room, and rushing in they found their little son sitting up in bed, terribly frightened. "What was the matter?"

"The White Lady! The White Lady!" cried the boy.

"What lady," asked the bewildered parents; "there is no lady here!"

"She is gone," replied the boy, "and she looked so angry because I would not go with her. She was a fine lady—and she sat down on my bedside and wrung her hands and cried sore; then she kissed me and asked me to go with her, and she would make me a rich man, as she had buried a large box of gold, many hundred years since, down in a vault, and she would give it me, as she could not rest so long as it was there. When I told her I durst not go, she said she would carry me, and was lifting me up when I cried out and frightened her away." When the boy grew up he invariably persisted in the truth of his statement, and at forty years of age could recall the scene so vividly as "to make him shudder, as if still he felt her cold lips press his cheeks and the death-like embrace of her wan arms."

Equally curious is the old tradition told of Lynton Castle, of which not a stone remains, although, once upon a time, it was as stately a stronghold as ever echoed to the clash of knightly arms. One evening there came to its gates a monk, who in the name of the Holy Virgin asked alms, but the lady of the Castle liked not his gloomy brow, and bade him begone. Resenting such treatment, the monk drew up his well-knit frame, and vowed:—"All that is thine shall be mine, until in the porch of the holy church, a lady and a child shall stand and beckon."

Little heed was taken of these ominous words, and as years passed by a baron succeeded to the Lynton estates, whose greed was such that he dared to lay his sacrilegious hand even upon holy treasures. But as he sate among his gold, the black monk entered, and summoned him to his fearful audit; and his servants, aroused by his screams, found only a lifeless corpse. This was considered retribution for his sins of the past, and his son, taking warning, girded on his sword, and in Palestine did doughty deeds against the Saracen. By his side was constantly seen the mysterious Black Monk—his friend and guide—but "at length the wine-cup and the smiles of lewd women lured him from the path of right." After a time the knight returned to Devonshire, "and lo, on the happy Sabbath morning, the chimes of the church-bells flung out their silver music on the air, and the memories of an innocent childhood woke up instantly in his sorrowing heart." In vain the Black Monk sought to beguile him from the holy fane, and whispered to him of bright eyes and a distant bower. He paused only for a moment. In the shadow of the porch stood the luminous forms of his mother and sister, who lifted up their spirit hands, and beckoned. The knight tore himself from the Black Monk's grasp and rushed towards them, exclaiming, "I come! I come! Mother, sister, I am saved! O, Heaven, have pity on me!" The story adds that the three were borne up in a radiant cloud, but "the Black Monk leapt headlong into the depths of the abyss beneath, and the castle fell to pieces with a sudden crash, and where its towers had soared statelily into the sunlit air was now outspread the very desolation—the valley of the rocks—" and thus the vow was accomplished, all that remains nowadays to remind the visitor of that stately castle and its surroundings being a lonely glen in the valley of rocks where a party of marauders, it is said, were once overtaken and slaughtered.

In some cases churches have been built in performance of vows, and at the Tichborne Trial one of the witnesses deposed how Sir Edward Doughty made a vow, when his son was ill, that if the child recovered he would build a church at Poole. Contrary to all expectation, the child "did recover most miraculously, for it had been ill beyond all hope, and Sir Edward built a church at Poole, and there it stands until this day." There are numerous stories of the same kind, and the peculiar position of the old church of St. Antony, in Kirrier, Cornwall, is accounted for by the following tradition: It is said that, soon after the Conquest, as some Normans of rank were crossing from Normandy into England, they were driven by a terrific storm on the Cornish coast, where they were in imminent danger of destruction. In their peril and distress they called on St. Antony, and made a vow that if he would preserve them from shipwreck they would build a church in his honour on the spot where they first landed. The vessel was wafted into the Durra Creek, and there the pious Normans, as soon as possible, fulfilled their vow. A similar tradition is told of Gunwalloe Parish Church, which, a local legend says, was erected as a votive offering by one who here escaped from shipwreck, for, "when he had miraculously escaped from the fury of the waves, he vowed that he would build a chapel in which the sounds of prayer and praise to God should blend with the never-ceasing voice of those waves from which he had but narrowly escaped. So near to the sea is the church, that at times it is reached by the waves, which have frequently washed away the walls of the churchyard." But vows of a similar nature have been connected with sacred buildings in most countries, and Vienna owes the church of St. Charles to a vow made by the Emperor Charles the Sixth during an epidemic. The silver ship, given by the Queen of St. Louis, was made in accordance with a vow. According to Joinville, the queen "said she wanted the king, to beg he would make some vows to God and the Saints, for the sailors around her were in the greatest danger of being drowned."

"'Madam,' I replied, 'vow to make a pilgrimage to my lord St. Nicholas at Varengeville, and I promise you that God will restore you in safety to France. At least, then, Madam, promise him that if God shall restore you in safety to France, you will give him a silver ship of the value of five masses; and if you shall do this, I assure you that, at the entreaty of St. Nicholas, God will grant you a successful voyage.' Upon this, she made a vow of a silver ship to St. Nicholas." Similarly, there was a statue at Venice said to have performed great miracles. A merchant vowed perpetual gifts of wax candles in gratitude for being saved by the light of a candle on a dark night, reminding us of Byron's description of a storm at sea, in 'Don Juan' (Canto II.):

"Some went to prayers again and made vowsOf candles to their saints."

Numerous vows of this kind are recorded, and it may be remembered how a certain Empress promised a golden lamp to the church of Notre Dame des Victoires, in the event of her husband coming safely out of the doctor's hands; and, as recently as the year 1867, attired in the garb of a pilgrim of the olden time, walked, in fulfilment of a vow, from Madrid to Rome when she fancied herself at death's door.

Many card-players and gamesters, unable to bear reverse, have made vows which they lacked the moral courage to keep. Dr. Norman Macleod tells a curious anecdote of a well-known character who lived in the parish of Sedgley, near Wolverhampton, and who, having lost a considerable sum of money by a match at cock-fighting—to which practice he was notoriously addicted—made a vow that he would never fight another cock as long as he lived, "frequently calling upon God to damn his soul to all eternity if he did, and, with dreadful imprecations, wishing the devil might fetch him if he ever made another bet."

For a time he adhered to his vow, but two years afterwards he was inspired with a violent desire to attend a cock-fight at Wolverhampton, and accordingly visited the place for that purpose. On reaching the scene he soon disregarded his vow, and cried: "I hold four to three on such a cock!"

"Four what?" said one of his companions.

"Four shillings," replied he.

"I'll lay," said the other, upon which they confirmed the wager, and, as his custom was, he threw down his hat and put his hand in his pocket for the money, when he instantly fell down dead. Terrified at the sight, "some who were present for ever after desisted from this infamous sport; but others proceeded in the barbarous diversion as soon as the dead body was removed from the spot."

Another inveterate gambler was Colonel Edgeworth, who on one occasion, having lost all his ready cash at the card tables, actually borrowed his wife's diamond earrings, and staking them had a fortunate turn of luck, rising a winner; whereupon he solemnly vowed never to touch cards or dice again. And yet, it is said, before the week was out, he was pulling straws from a rick, and betting upon which should prove the longest. On the other hand, Tate Wilkinson relates an interesting anecdote of John Wesley who in early life was very fond of a game of whist, and every Saturday was one of a constant party at a rubber, not only for the afternoon, but also for the evening. But the last Saturday that he ever played at cards the rubber at whist was longer than he expected, and, "on observing the tediousness of the game he pulled out his watch, and to his shame he found it was some minutes past eight, which was beyond the time he had appointed for the Lord. He thought the devil had certainly tempted him beyond his hour, he suddenly therefore gave up his cards to a gentleman near him to finish the game," and left the room, making a vow never to play with "the devil's pages," as he called them, again. That vow he never broke.

Political vows, as is well known, have a curious history, and an interesting incident is told in connection with one of the ancestors of Sir Walter Scott. It appears that Walter Scott, the first of Raeburn, by Ann Isabel, his wife, daughter of William Macdougall, had two sons, William, direct ancestor of the Lairds of Raeburn, and Walter, progenitor of the Scotts of Abbotsford. The younger, who was generally known by the curious appellation of "Bearded Watt," from a vow which he had made to leave his beard unshaven until the restoration of the Stuarts, reminds us of those Servian patriots who during the bombardment of Belgrade thirty years ago, made a vow that they would never allow a razor to touch their faces until the thing could be done in the fortress itself. Five years afterwards, in 1867, the Servians marched through the streets of Belgrade, with enormous beards, preceded by the barbers, each with razor in hand, and entered the fortresses to have the last office of the vow performed on them.

FOOTNOTES:

[12] Agnes Strickland, "Lives of the Queens of England," 1884, iii., 454-5.

[13] See Sir Walter Scott's notes to the "Bride of Lammermoor."

[14] Harland's "Lancashire Legends," 1882, p. 263-4.

CHAPTER IV.
STRANGE BANQUETS.

"O'Rourke's noble feast will ne'er be forgot
By those who were there—or those who were not."

In the above words the Dean of St. Patrick has immortalised an Irish festival of the eighteenth century; and some such memory will long cling to many a family or historic banquet, which—like the tragic one depicted in "Macbeth," where the ghost of the murdered Banquo makes its uncanny appearance, or that remarkable feast described by Lord Lytton, where Zanoni drinks with impunity the poisoned cup, remarking to the Prince, "I pledge you even in this wine"—has been the scene of some unusual, or extraordinary occurrence.

At one time or another, the wedding feast has witnessed many a strange and truly romantic occurrence, in some instances the result of unrequited love, or faithless pledges, as happened at the marriage feast of the second Viscount Cullen. At the early age of sixteen he had been betrothed to Elizabeth Trentham, a great heiress; but in the course of his travels abroad he formed a strong attachment to an Italian lady of rank, whom he afterwards deserted for his first betrothed. In due time arrangements were made for their marriage; but on the eventful day, while the wedding party were feasting in the great hall at Rushton, a strange carriage, drawn by six horses, drew up, and forth stepped a dark lady, who, at once entering the hall and, seizing a goblet—"to punish his falsehood and pride"—to the astonishment of all present, drank perdition to the bridegroom, and, having uttered a curse upon his bride, to the effect that she would live in wretchedness and die in want, promptly disappeared to be traced no further.

No small consternation was caused by this unlooked-for contretemps; but the young Viscount made light of it to his fair bride, dispelling her alarm by explanations which satisfied her natural curiosity. But, it is said, in after days, this unpleasant episode created an unfavourable impression in her mind, and at times made her give way to feelings of a despondent character. As events turned out, the curse of her marriage day was in a great measure fulfilled. It is true she became a prominent beauty of the Court of Charles II., and was painted with less than his usual amount of drapery by

Sir Peter Lely. It is recorded also, that she twice gave an asylum to Monmouth, in the room at Rushton, still known as the "Duke's Room"; but, living unhappily with her husband, she died, notwithstanding her enormous fortune, in comparative penury, at Kettering, at a great age, as recently as the year 1713.

A curious tale of love and deception is told of Bulgaden Hall, once—according to Ferrers, in his "History of Limerick"—the most magnificent seat in the South of Ireland—erected by the Right Hon. George Evans, who was created Baron Carbery, County of Cork, on the 9th of May, 1715. A family tradition proclaims him to have been noted for great personal attractions, so much so, that Queen Anne, struck by his appearance, took a ring from her finger at one of her levees, and presented it to him—a ring preserved as a heir-loom at Laxton Hall, Northamptonshire. In 1741, he married Grace, the daughter, and eventually heiress of Sir Ralph Freke, of Castle Freke, in the County of Cork, by whom he had four sons and the same number of daughters; and it was George Evans, the eldest son and heir, who became the chief personage in the following extraordinary marriage fraud.

It appears that at an early age he fell in love with the beautiful daughter of his host, Colonel Stamer, who was only too ready to sanction such an alliance. But, despite the brilliant prospects which this contemplated marriage opened to the young lady, she turned a deaf ear to any mention of it, for she loved another. As far as her parents could judge she seemed inexorable, and they could only allay the suspense of the expectant lover by assuring him that their daughter's "natural timidity alone prevented an immediate answer to his suit."

But what their feelings of surprise were on the following day can be imagined, when Miss Stamer announced to her parents her willingness to marry George Evans. It was decided that there should be no delay, and the marriage day was at once fixed. At this period of our social life, the wedding banquet was generally devoted to wine and feasting, while the marriage itself did not take place till the evening. And, according to custom, sobriety at these bridal feasts was, we are told, "a positive violation of all good breeding, and the guests would have thought themselves highly dishonoured had the bridegroom escaped scathless from the wedding banquet."

Accordingly, half unconscious of passing events, George Evans was conducted to the altar, where the marriage knot was indissolubly tied. But, as soon as he had recovered from the effects of the bridal feast, he discovered, to his intense horror and dismay, that the bride he had taken was not the woman of his choice—in short, he was the victim of a cheat.

Indignant at this cruel imposture, he ascertained that the plot emanated from the woman who, till then, had been the ideal of his soul, and that she had substituted her veiled sister Anne for herself at the altar. The remainder of this strange affair is briefly told:—George Evans had one, and only one, interview with his wife, and thus addressed her in the following words: "Madam, you have attained your end. I need not say how you bear my name; and, for the sake of your family, I acknowledge you as my wife. You shall receive an income from me suitable to your situation. This, probably, is all you cared for with regard to me, and you and I shall meet no more in this world."

"MADAM, YOU HAVE ATTAINED YOUR END.
YOU AND I SHALL MEET NO MORE IN THIS WORLD."

He would allow no explanation, and almost immediately left his home and country, never to meet again the woman who had so basely betrayed him. The glory of Bulgaden Hall was gone. Its young master, in order to quench his sorrow and bury his disgust, gave way to every kind of dissipation, and died its victim in 1769. And, writes Sir Bernard Burke, "from the period of its desertion by its luckless master, Bulgaden Hall gradually sank into ruin; and to mark its site nought remains but the foundation walls and a solitary stone, bearing the family arms."

A strange incident, of which, it is said, no satisfactory explanation has ever yet been forthcoming, happened during the wedding banquet of Alexander III. at Jedburgh Castle, a weird and gruesome episode which Edgar Poe expanded into his "Masque of the Red Death." The story goes that in the midst of the festivities, a mysterious figure glided amongst the astonished guests—tall and gaunt, and shrouded from head to foot in the habiliments of the grave, the mask which concealed the visage resembling the countenance of a stiffened corpse.

"Who dares," demands the royal host, "to insult us with this blasphemous mockery? Seize him and unmask him, that we may know whom we have to hang at sunrise from the battlements."

But when the awe-struck revellers took courage and grasped the figure, "they gasped in unutterable horror on finding the grave cerements and corpse-like mask, which they handled with so violent a rudeness, untenanted by any tangible form, vanishing as suddenly as it had appeared." All sorts of theories have been suggested to account for this mysterious figure, but no satisfactory solution has been forthcoming, an incident of which, it may be remembered, Heywood has given a graphic picture:

In the mid-revels, the first ominous nightOf their espousals, when the room shone brightWith lighted tapers—the king and queen leadingThe curious measures, lords and ladies treadingThe self-same strains—the king looks back by chanceAnd spies a strange intruder fill the dance,Namely, a mere anatomy, quite bare,His naked limbs both without flesh and hair(As he deciphers Death), who stalks about,Keeping true measure till the dance be out.

Inexplicable, however, as the presence of this unearthly, mysterious personage was felt to be by all engaged in the marriage revels, it was regarded as the forerunner of some approaching catastrophe. Prophets and seers lost no time in turning the affair to their own interest, and amongst them Thomas the Rhymer predicted that the 16th of March would be "the stormiest day that ever was witnessed in Scotland." But when the supposed ill-fated day arrived, it was the very reverse of stormy, being still and mild, and public opinion began to ridicule the prophetic utterance of Thomas the Rhymer, when, to the amazement and consternation of all, there came the appalling news, "The king is dead," whereupon Thomas the Rhymer ejaculated, "That is the storm which I meant, and there was never tempest which will bring to Scotland more ill-luck."

The disappearance of the heir to a property, which has always been a favourite subject with novelists and romance writers, has occasionally happened in real life, and a Shropshire legend relates how, long ago, the heir of the house of Corbet went away to the wars, and remained absent so many years that his family—as in the case of Enoch Arden—gave up all hope of ever seeing him again, and eventually mourned for him as dead. His younger brother succeeded to the property, and prepared to take to himself a wife, and reign in the old family hall.

But on the wedding day, in the midst of the feasting, a pilgrim came to the gate asking hospitality and alms. He was bidden to sit down and share the feast, but scarcely was the banquet ended when the pilgrim revealed himself as the long lost elder brother. The disconcerted bridegroom acknowledged him at once, but the latter generously resigned the greater part of the estates to his brother, and, sooner than mar the prospects of the newly married couple, he lived a life of obscurity upon one small manor. There seems, however, to be a very small basis of fact for this story. The Corbets of Shropshire—one branch of whom are owners of Moreton Corbet—are among the very oldest of the many old Shropshire families. They trace their descent back to Corbet the Norman, whose sons, Robert and Roger, appear in Domesday Book as holding large estates under Roger, Earl of Shrewsbury. The grandsons of Roger Corbet were Thomas Corbet of Wattlesborough, and Robert Corbet. Thomas, who was evidently the elder of the two, it seems went beyond seas, leaving his lands in the custody of his brother Robert. Both brothers left descendants, but the elder branch of the family never attained to such rank and prosperity as the younger one." Hence, perhaps, the origin of the legend; but Moreton Corbet did not come into the possession of the family till long after this date.[15]

Whatever truth there may be in this old tradition, there is every reason to believe that some of the worst tragedies recorded in family history have been due to jealousy; and an extraordinary instance of such unnatural feeling was that displayed by the second wife of Sir Robert Scott, of Thirlestane, one of the most distinguished cadets of the great House of Buccleuch. Distracted with mortification that her husband's rich inheritance would descend to his son by his first wife, she secretly resolved to compass the destruction of her step-son, and determined to execute her hateful purpose at the festivities held in honour of the young laird's twentieth birthday. Having taken into her confidence one John Lally, the family piper, this wretched man procured three adders, from which he selected the parts replete with the most deadly poison, and, after grinding them to fine powder, Lady Thirlestane mixed them in a bottle of wine. Previous to the commencement of the birthday feast, the young laird having called for wine to drink the healths of the workmen who had just completed the mason work of the new Castle of Gamescleugh—his future residence—the piper Lally filled a silver cup from the poisoned bottle, which the ill-fated youth hastily drank off. So potent was the poison that the young laird died within an hour, and a feeling of horror seized the birthday guests as to who could have done so foul a deed. But the father seems to have had his suspicions, and having caused a bugle to be blown, as a signal for all the family to assemble in the castle court, he inquired, "Are we all here?"

A voice answered, "All but the piper, John Lally!"

These words, it is said, sounded like a knell in Sir Robert's ear, and the truth was manifest to him. But unwilling to make a public example of his own wife, he adopted a somewhat unique method of vengeance, and publicly proclaimed that as he could not bestow the estate on his son while alive, he would spend it upon him when dead. Accordingly, the body of his son was embalmed with the most costly drugs, and lay in state for a year and a day, during which time Sir Robert kept open house, feasting all who chose to be his guests; Lady Thirlestane meanwhile being imprisoned in a vault of the castle, and fed upon bread and water. "During the last three days of this extraordinary feast", writes Sir Bernard Burke,[16] "the crowds were immense. It was as if the whole of the south of Scotland was assembled at Thirlestane. Butts of the richest and rarest wine were carried into the fields, their ends were knocked out with hatchets, and the liquor was carried about in stoups. The burn of Thirlestane literally ran with wine." Sir Robert died soon afterwards, and left his family in utter destitution, his wife dying in absolute beggary. Thus was avenged the crime of this cruel and unprincipled woman, whose fatal jealousy caused the ruin of the family.

Political intrigue, again, has been the origin of many an act of treachery, done under the semblance of hospitality, or given rise to strange incidents.

To go back to early times, it seems that Edward the Confessor had long indulged a suspicion that Earl Godwin—who had in the first instance accused Queen Emma of having caused the death of her son—was himself implicated in that transaction. It so happened that the King and a large concourse of prelates and nobility were holding a large dinner at Winchester, in honour of the Easter festival, when the butler, in bringing in a dish, slipped, but recovered his balance by making adroit use of his other foot.

"Thus does brother assist brother," exclaimed Earl Godwin, thinking to be witty at the butler's expense.

"And thus might I have been now assisted by my Alfred, if Earl Godwin had not prevented it," replied the King: for the Earl's remark had recalled to his mind the suspicion he had long entertained of the Earl having been concerned in Prince Alfred's death.

Resenting the king's words, the Earl holding up the morsel which he was about to eat, uttered a great oath, and in the name of God expressed a wish that the morsel might choke him if he had in any way been concerned in that murder. Accordingly he there and then put the morsel into his mouth, and attempted to swallow it; but his efforts were in vain, it stuck fast in his throat—immovable upward or downward—his respiration failed, his eyes became fixed, his countenance convulsed, and in a minute more he fell dead under the table.

Edward, convinced of the Earl's guilt, and seeing divine justice manifested, and remembering, it is said, with bitterness the days past when he had given a willing ear to the calumnies spread about his innocent mother, cried out, in an indignant voice, "Carry away that dog, and bury him in the high road." But the body was deposited by the Earl's cousin in the cathedral.

Several accounts have been written of that terrible banquet, to which the Earl of Douglas was invited by Sir Alexander Livingstone and the Chancellor Crichton—who craftily dissembled their intentions—to sup at the royal table in the Castle of Edinburgh. The Earl was foolhardy enough to accept the ill-fated invitation, and shortly after he had taken his place at the festive board, the head of a black bull—the certain omen, in those days in Scotland, of immediate death—was placed on the table. The Earl, anticipating treachery, instantly sprang to his feet, and lost no time in making every effort to escape. But no chance was given him to do so, and with his younger brother he was hurried along into the courtyard of the castle, and after being subjected to a mock trial, he was beheaded "in the back court of the castle that lieth to the west". The death of the young earl, and his untimely fate, were the subjects of lament in one of the ballads of the time.

"Edinburgh castle, town, and tower,God grant them sink for sin;And that even for the black dinnerEarl Douglas gat therein."

This emphatic malediction is cited by Hume of Godscroft in his "History of the House of Douglas," as referring to William, sixth Earl of Douglas, a youth of eighteen; and Hume, speaking of this transaction, says, with becoming indignation: "It is sure the people did abhorre it—execrating the very place where it was done, in detestation of the fact—of which the memory remaineth yet to our dayes in these words."

Many similar stories are recorded in the history of the past, the worst form of treachery oftentimes lurking beneath the festive cup, and in times of commotion, when suspicion and mistrust made men feel insecure even when entertained in the banqueting hall of some powerful host, it is not surprising that great persons had their food tasted by those who were supposed to have made themselves acquainted with its wholesomeness. But this practice could not always afford security when the taster was ready to sacrifice his own life, as in King John (act v. sc. 6):

HUBERT. The king, I fear, is poisoned by a monk:
I left him almost speechless.
BASTARD. How did he take it? Who did taste to him?
HUBERT. A monk, I tell you; a resolved villain.

But, in modern days, one of the most unnatural tragedies on record was the murder of Sir John Goodere, Foote's maternal uncle, by his brother Captain Goodere, a naval officer. In the year 1740, the two brothers dined at a friend's house near Bristol. For a long time they had been on bad terms, owing to certain money transactions, but at the dinner table a reconciliation was, to all appearance, made between them. But it was a most terrible piece of underhand treachery, for on leaving that dinner table, Sir John was waylaid on his return home by some men from his brother's vessel—acting by his brother's authority—carried on board, and deliberately strangled; Captain Goodere not only unconcernedly looking on, but actually furnishing the rope with which this fearful crime was committed. One of the strangest parts of this terrible tale, Foote used to relate, was the fact that on the night the murder was committed he arrived at his father's house in Truro, and was kept awake for some time by the softest and sweetest strains of music he had ever heard. At first he fancied it might be a serenade got up by some of the family to welcome him home, but not being able to discover any trace of the musicians, he came to the conclusion that he was deceived by his own imagination. Shortly afterwards, however, he learnt that the murder had been committed at the same hour of the same night as he had been haunted by the mysterious sounds. In after days, he often spoke of this curious occurrence, regarding it as a supernatural warning, a conviction which he retained till his death.

But, strange and varied as are the scenes that have taken place at the banquet, whether great or small, such acts of fratricide have been rare, although, according to a family tradition relating to Osbaldeston Hall, a similar tragedy once happened at a family banquet. There is one room in the old hall whose walls are smeared with several red marks, which, it is said, can never be obliterated. These stains have some resemblance to blood, and are generally supposed to have been caused when, many years ago, one of the family was brutally murdered. The story commonly current is that there was once a great family gathering at Osbaldeston Hall, at which every member of the family was present. The feast passed off satisfactorily, and the liquor was flowing freely round, when, unfortunately, family differences began to be discussed. These soon caused angry recriminations, and at length two of the company challenged each other to mortal combat. Friends interfered, and, by the judicious intervention on their part, the quarrel seemed to be made up. But soon afterwards the two accidentally met in this room, and Thomas Osbaldeston drew his sword and murdered his brother-in-law without resistance. For this crime he was deemed a felon, and forfeited his lands. Ever since that ill-fated day the room has been haunted. Tradition says that the ghost of the murdered man continues to haunt the scene of the conflict, and during the silent hours of the night it may be seen passing from the room with uplifted hands, and with the appearance of blood streaming from a wound in the breast.[17]

But, turning to incidents of a less tragic nature, an amusing story is told of the Earl of Hopetoun, who, when he could not induce a certain Scottish laird, named Dundas, to sell his old family residence known as "The Tower," which was on the very verge of his own beautiful pleasure grounds, tried to lead him on to a more expensive style of living than that to which he had been accustomed, thinking thereby he might run into debt, and be compelled to sell his property.

Accordingly, Dundas was frequently invited to Hopetoun House, and on one occasion his lordship invited himself and a fashionable shooting party to "The Tower," "congratulating himself on the hole which a few dinners like this would make in the old laird's rental." But, as soon as the covers were removed from the dishes, no small chagrin was caused to Lord Hopetoun and his friends when their eyes rested on "a goodly array of alternate herrings and potatoes spread from the top to the bottom," Dundas at the same time inviting his guests to pledge him in a bumper of excellent whiskey. Drinking jocularly to his lordship's health, he humorously said, "It won't do, my lord; it won't do! But, whenever you or your guests will honour my poor hall of Stang Hill Tower with your presence at this hour, I promise you no worse fare than now set before you, the best and fattest salt herrings that the Forth can produce, and the strongest mountain dew. To this I beg that your lordship and your honoured friends may do ample justice."

It is needless to say that Lord Hopetoun never dined again at Stang Hill Tower but some time after, when Dundas was on his death-bed, he advised his son to make the best terms he could with Lord Hopetoun, remarking, "He will, sooner or later, have our little property." An exchange was made highly advantageous to the Dundas family, the estate of Aithrey being made over to them.[18]

A curious and humorous narrative is told of General Dalzell, a noted persecutor of the Covenanters. In the course of his Continental service he had been brought into the immediate circle of the German Court, and one day had the honour to be a guest at a splendid Imperial banquet, where, as a part of his state, the German Emperor was waited on by the great feudal dignitaries of the empire, one of whom was the Duke of Modena, the head of the illustrious house of Este. After his appointment by Charles II. as

Commander-in-Chief in Scotland, he was invited by the Duke of York—afterwards James II., and then residing at Holyrood—to dine with him and the Duchess, Princess May of Modena. But as this was, we are told, what might be called a family dinner, the Duchess demurred to the General being admitted to such an honour, whereupon he naively replied that this was not his first introduction to the house of Este, for that he had known her Royal Highness's father, the Duke of Modena, and that he had stood behind his chair, while he sat by the Emperor's side.

There was another kind of banquet, in which it has been remarked the defunct had the principal honours, having the same ceremonious respect paid to his waxen image as though he were alive. Thus we are reminded how the famous Henrietta, Duchess of Marlborough demonstrated her appreciation for Congreve in a most extraordinary manner. Report goes that she had his figure made in wax, talked to it as if it had been alive, placed it at the table with her, took every care that it was supplied with different sorts of meat, and, in short, the same formalities were, throughout, scrupulously observed in these weird and strange repasts, just as if Congreve himself had been present.

Saint Foix, it may be remembered, who wrote in the time of Louis XIV., has left an interesting account of the ceremonial after the death of a King of France, during the forty days before the funeral, when his wax effigy lay in state. It appears that the royal officers served him at meals as though he were still alive, the maître d'hotel handed the napkin to the highest lord present to be delivered to the king, a prelate blessed the table, and the basins of water were handed to the royal armchair. Grace was said in the accustomed manner, save that there was added to it the "De Profundis." We cannot be surprised that such strange proceedings as these gave rise to much ridicule, and helped to bring the Court itself into contempt.

FOOTNOTES:

[15] Miss Jackson's "Shropshire Folklore," 101.

[16] Family Romance, 1853, pp. 1-8.

[17] Harland's "Lancashire Legends," 271-2.

[18] Sir Bernard Burke, "Family Romance," 1853, I., 307-12.

CHAPTER V.
MYSTERIOUS ROOMS.

> A jolly place, said he, in days of old;
> But something ails it now—the spot is curst.
>
> WORDSWORTH.

A peculiar feature of many old country houses is the so-called "strange room," around which the atmosphere of mystery has long clung. In certain cases, such rooms have gained an unenviable notoriety from having been the scene, in days gone by, of some tragic occurrence, the memory of which has survived in the local legend, or tradition. The existence, too, of such rooms has supplied the novelist with the most valuable material for the construction of those plots in which the mysterious element holds a prominent place. Historical romance, again, with its tales of adventure, has invested numerous rooms with a grim aspect, and caused the imagination to conjure up all manner of weird and unearthly fancies concerning them. Walpole, for instance, writing of Berkeley Castle, says: "The room shown for the murder of Edward II., and the shrieks of an agonising king, I verily believe to be genuine. It is a dismal chamber, almost at the top of the house, quite detached, and to be approached only by a kind of footbridge, and from that descends a large flight of steps that terminates on strong gates, exactly a situation for a corps de garde." And speaking of Edward's imprisonment here, may be mentioned the pathetic story told by Sir Richard Baker, in his usual odd, circumstantial manner: "When Edward II. was taken by order of his Queen and carried to Berkeley Castle, to the end that he should not be known, they shaved his head and beard, and that in a most beastly manner; for they took him from his horse and set him upon a hillock, and then, taking puddle water out of a ditch thereby, they went to wash him, his barber telling him that the cold water must serve for this time; whereat the miserable king, looking sternly upon him, said that whether they would or no he would have warm water to wash him, and therewithal, to make good his word, he presently shed forth a shower of tears. Never was king turned out of a kingdom in such a manner." And there can be no doubt that many of the rooms which have attracted notice on account of their architectural peculiarities, were purposely designed for concealment in times of political commotion. Of the numerous stories told of the mysterious death of Lord Lovel, one informs us[19] how, on the demolition of a very old house—formerly the patrimony of the Lovel's—

about a century ago, there was found in a small chamber, so secret that the farmer who inhabited the house knew it not, the remains of an immured being, and such remnants of barrels and jars as appeared to justify the idea of that chamber having been used as a place of refuge for the lord of the mansion; and that after consuming the stores which he had provided in case of a disastrous event, he died unknown even to his servants and tenants. But the circumstances attending Lord Lovell's death have always been matter of conjecture, and in the "Annals of England," another version of the story is given:[20] "Lord Lovel is believed to have escaped from the field, and to have lived for a while in concealment at Minster Lovel, Oxfordshire, but at length to have been starved to death through the neglect or treachery of an attendant."

At Broughton Castle there is a curiously designed room, which, at one time or another, has attracted considerable attention. According to Lord Nugent, in his "Memorials of Hampden," this room is "so contrived, by being surrounded by thick stone walls, and casemated, that no sound from within can be heard. The chamber appears to have been built about the time of King John, and is reported, on very doubtful grounds of tradition, to have been the room used for the sittings of the Puritans." And, he adds: "It seems an odd fancy, although a very prevailing one, to suppose that wise men, employed in capital matters of state, must needs choose the most mysterious and suspicious retirements for consultation, instead of the safer and less remarkable expedient of a walk in the open fields." It was probably in this room that the secret meetings of Hampden and his confederates were held, which Anthony à Wood thus describes: "Several years before the Civil War began, Lord Sage, being looked upon as the godfather of that party, had meetings of them in his house at Broughton, where was a room and passage thereunto, which his servants were prohibited to come near. And when they were of a complete number, there would be a great noise and talkings heard among them, to the admiration of those that lived in the house, yet never could they discern their lord's companions."

Amongst other secret rooms which have their historical associations, are those at Hendlip Hall, near Worcester. This famous residence—which has scarcely a room that is not provided with some means of escape—is commonly reported to have been built by John Abingdon in the reign of Queen Elizabeth, this personage having been a zealous partisan of Mary Queen of Scots. It was here also, under the care of Mr. and Mrs. Abingdon, that Father Garnet was concealed for several weeks in the winter of 1605-6, but who eventually paid the penalty of his guilty knowledge of the Gunpowder Plot. A hollow in the wall of Mrs. Abingdon's bedroom was covered up, and there was a narrow crevice into which a reed was laid, so that soup and wine could be passed by her into the recess, without the fact being noticed from any other room. But the Government, suspecting that some of the Gunpowder Conspirators were concealed at Hendlip Hall, sent Sir Henry Bromley, of Holt Castle, a justice of the peace, with the most minute orders, which are very funny: "In the search," says the document, "first observe the parlour where they use to dine and sup; in the last part of that parlour it is conceived there is some vault, which to discover, you must take care to draw down the wainscot, whereby the entry into the vault may be discovered. The lower parts of the house must be tried with a broach, by putting the same into the ground some foot or two, to try whether there may be perceived some timber, which if there be, there must be some vault underneath it. For the upper rooms you must observe whether they be more in breadth than the lower rooms, and look in which places the rooms must be enlarged, by pulling out some boards you may discover some vaults. Also, if it appear that there be some corners to the chimneys, and the same boarded, if the boards be taken away there will appear some secret place. If the walls seem to be thick and covered with wainscot, being tried with a gimlet, if it strike not the wall but go through, some suspicion is to be had thereof. If there be any double loft, some two or three feet, one above another, in such places any person may be harboured privately. Also, if there be a loft towards the roof of the house, in which there appears no entrance out of any other place or lodging, it must of necessity be opened and looked into, for these be ordinary places of hovering (hiding)."

The house was searched from garret to cellar without any discovery being made, and Mrs. Abingdon, feigning to be angry with the searchers, shut herself up in her bedroom day and night, eating and drinking there, by which means through the secret tube she fed Father Garnet and another Jesuit father. But after a protracted search of ten days, these two men surrendered themselves, pressed, it is said, "for the need of air rather than food, for marmalade and other sweetmeats were found in their den, and they had warm and nutritive drinks passed to them by the reed through the chimney," as already described. This historic mansion, it may be added, on account of its elevated position, was capitally adapted as a place of concealment, for "it afforded the means of keeping a watchful look-out for the approach of the emissaries of the law, or of persons by whom it might have been dangerous for any skulking priest to be seen, supposing his reverence to have gone forth for an hour to take the air."

Another important instance of a strange room is that existing at Ingatestone Hall, in Essex, which was, in years gone by, a summer residence belonging to the Abbey of Barking. It came with the estate into possession of the family of Petre in the reign of Henry VIII., and continued to be occupied as their family seat until the latter half of the last century. In the south-east corner of a small room attached to what was probably the host's bedroom, there was discovered some years ago a mysterious hiding place—fourteen feet long, two feet broad, and ten feet high. On some floor-boards being removed, a hole or trap door—about two feet square—was found, with a twelve-foot ladder, to descend into the room below, the floor of which was composed of nine inches of dry sand. This, on being examined, brought to light a few bones which, it has been suggested, are the remains of food supplied to some unfortunate occupant during confinement. But the existence of this secret room must, it is said, have been familiar to the heads of the family for several generations, evidence of this circumstance being afforded by a packing case which was found in this hidden retreat, and upon which was the following direction: "For the Right Honble the Lady Petre, at Ingatestone Hall, in Essex." The wood, also, was in a decayed state, and the writing in an antiquated style, which is only what might be expected considering that the Petre family left Ingatestone Hall between the years 1770 and 1780.

There are numerous rooms of this curious description which, it must be remembered, were, in many cases, the outcome of religious intolerance in the sixteenth century, and early in the seventeenth, when the celebration of Mass in this country was forbidden. Hence those families that persisted in adhering to the Roman Catholic faith oftentimes kept a priest, who celebrated it in a room—opening whence was a secret one, to which in case of emergency he could retreat. Evelyn in his Diary, speaking of Ham House, at Weybridge, belonging to the Duke of Norfolk, as having some of these secret rooms, writes: "My lord, leading me about the house, made no scruple of showing me all the hiding places for Popish priests, and where they said Masse, for he was no bigoted papist." The old Manor House at Dinsdale-upon-Tees has a secret room, which is very cleverly situated at the top of the staircase, to which access is gained from above. The compartment is not very large, and is between two bedrooms, and alongside of the fireplace of one of them. "It would be a very snug place when the fire was lighted," writes a correspondent of "Notes and Queries," "and very secure, as it is necessary to enter the cockloft by a trap door at the extreme end of the building, and then crawl along under the roof into the hiding-place by a second trap-door." Among further instances of these curious relics of the past may be mentioned Armscott Manor, two or three miles distant from Shipston-on-Stour. According to a local tradition, George Fox at one time lived here. In a passage at the top of the house is the entrance to a secret room, which receives light from a small window in one of the gables, and in this room George Fox is said to have been concealed during the period he was persecuted by the county magistrates.

But sometimes such rooms furthered the designs of those who abetted and connived at deeds that would not bear the light, and Southey records an anecdote which is a good illustration of the bad uses to which they were probably often put: "At Bishop's Middleham, a man died with the reputation of a water drinker; and it was discovered that he had killed himself by secret drunkenness. There was a Roman Catholic hiding place, the entrance to which was from his bedroom. He converted it into a cellar, and the quantity of brandy which he had consumed was ascertained." Indeed, it is impossible to say to what ends these secret rooms were occasionally devoted; and there is little doubt but that they were the scenes of many of those thrilling stories upon which many of our local traditions have been founded.

Political refugees, too, were not infrequently secreted in these hiding places, and in the Manor House, Trent, near Sherborne, there is a strangely constructed chamber, entered from one of the upper rooms through a sliding panel in the oak wainscoting, in which tradition tells us Charles II. lay concealed for a fortnight on his escape to the coast, after the battle of Worcester. And Boscobel House, which also afforded Charles II. a safe retreat, has two secret chambers; and there are indications which point to the former existence of a third. The hiding place in which the King was hidden is situated in the squire's bedroom. It appears there was formerly a sliding panel in the wainscot, near the fireplace, which, when opened, gave access to a closet, the false floor of which still admits of a person taking up his position in this secret nook. The wainscoting, too, which concealed the movable panel in the bedroom was originally covered with tapestry, with which the room was hung. A curious story is told of Street Place, an old house, a mile and a half north of Plumpton, in the neighbourhood of Lewes, which dates from the time of James I., and was the seat of the Dobells. Behind the great chimney-piece of the hall was a deep recess, used for purposes of concealment; and it is said that one day a cavalier horseman, hotly pursued by some troopers, broke into the hall, spurred his horse into the recess, and disappeared for ever.

Bistmorton Court, an old moated manor house in the Malvern district, has a cunningly contrived secret room, which is opened by means of a spring, and this hidden nook is commonly reported to have played an important part in the War of the Roses, when numerous persons were concealed there at this troublous period. And a curious discovery was made some years ago at Danby Hall, in Wensleydale, Yorkshire, when, on a small secret room being brought to light, it was found to contain arms and saddlery for a troop of forty or fifty horse. It is generally supposed that these weapons had been hidden away in readiness for the Jacobite rising of 1715 or 1745.

In certain cases it would appear that, for some reason or other, the hiding place has been specially kept a secret among members of the family.

In the north of England there is Netherall, near Maryport, Cumberland, the seat of the old family of Senhouse. In this old mansion there is said to be a veritable secret room, its exact position in the house being known but to two persons—the heir-at-law and the family solicitor. It is affirmed that never has the secret of this hidden room been revealed to more than two living persons at a time. This mysterious room has no window, and, despite every endeavour to discover it, has successfully defied the ingenuity of even visitors staying in the house. This Netherall tradition is very similar to the celebrated one connected with Glamis Castle, the seat of Lord Strathmore, only in the latter case the secret room possesses a window, which, nevertheless, has not led to its identification. It is known as the "secret room" of the castle, and, although every other part of the castle has been satisfactorily explored, the search for this famous room has been in vain. None are supposed to be acquainted with its locality save Lord Strathmore, his heir, and the factor of the estate, who are bound not to reveal it unless to their successors in the secret. Many weird stories have clustered round this remarkable room; one legend connected with which has been thus described:

The castle now again behold,Then mark yon lofty turret bold,Which frowns above the western wing,Its grim walls darkly shadowing.There is a room within that towerNo mortal dare approach; the powerOf an avenging God is there.Dread—awfully display'd—beware!And enter not that dreadful room,Else yours may be a fearful doom.

According to one legendary romance—founded on an incident which is said to have occurred during one of the carousals of the Earl of Crawford, otherwise styled "Earl Beardie" or the "Tiger Earl"—there was many years ago a grand "meet" at Glamis, as the result of which many a noble deer lay dead upon the hill, and many a grizzly boar dyed with his heart's blood the rivers of the plain. As the day drew to its close, "the wearied huntsmen, with their fair attendants, returned, 'midst the sounds of martial music and the low whispered roundelays of the ladies, victorious to the castle." In the old baronial dining hall was spread a sumptuous and savoury feast, at which "venison and reeking game, rich smoked ham and savoury roe, flanked by the wild boar's head, and viands and pasties without name, blent profusely on the hospitable board, while jewelled and capacious goblets, filled with ruby wine, were lavishly handed round to the admiring guests."

At the completion of the banquet, the minstrel strung his ancient harp, and soon the company tripped lightly on the oaken floor, till the rafters rang with the merry sounds of their midnight revelry. For three days and nights the hunt and the feast continued, and as, at last, the revelries drew to a close, still four dark chieftains remained in the inner chamber of the castle, "and sang, and drank, and shouted, right merrilie. The day broke, yet louder rang the wassail roar; the goblets were over and over again replenished, and the terrible oaths and ribald songs continued, and the dice rattled, and the revelry became louder still, till the many walls of the old castle shook and reverberated with the awful sounds of debauchery, blasphemy, and crime."

"At length their wild, ungovernable frenzy reached its climax. They had drunk until their eyes had grown dim, and their hands could scarcely hold the hellish dice, when, driven by expiring fury, with fiendish glee, they defiantly gnashed their teeth and cursed the God of heaven! Then, with returning strength, and exhausting its last and fitful energies in still louder imprecations and more fearful yells, they deliberately and with unanimous voice consigned their guilty souls to the nethermost hell! Fatal words! In a bright, broad sheet of lurid and sulphurous flame the Prince of Darkness appeared in their midst, and struck—not the shaft of death, but the vitality of eternal life—and there to this day in that dreaded room they sit, transfixed in all their hideous expression of ghastly terror and dismay—doomed to drink the wine cup and throw the dice till the dawning of the Great Judgment Day."[21]

Another explanation of the mystery is that during one of the feuds between the Lindsays and the Ogilvies, a number of the latter Clan, flying from their enemies, came to Glamis Castle, and begged hospitality of the owner. He admitted them, and on the plea of hiding them, he secured them all in this room, and then left them to starve. Their bones, it is averred, lie there to this day, the sight of which, it has been stated, so appalled the late Lord Strathmore on entering the room, that he had it walled up. Some assert that, owing to some hereditary curse, like those described in a previous chapter, at certain intervals a kind of vampire is born into the family of the Strathmore Lyons, and that as no one would like to destroy this monstrosity, it is kept concealed till its term of life is run. But, whatever the mystery may be, such rooms, like the locked chamber of Blue Beard, are not open to vulgar gaze, a circumstance which has naturally perpetuated the curiosity attached to them. The reputation, too, which Glamis Castle has long had for possessing so strange a room has led to a host of the most gruesome stories being circulated in connection with it, many of which from time to time have appeared in print. According to one account,[22] "a lady, very well known in London society, an artistic and social celebrity, went to stay at Glamis Castle for the first time. She was allotted very handsome apartments just on the point of junction between the new buildings—perhaps a hundred or two hundred years old—and the very ancient part of the castle. The rooms were handsomely furnished; no grim tapestry swung to and fro, all was smooth, easy, and modern, and the guest retired to bed without a thought of the mysteries of Glamis. In the morning she appeared at the breakfast table cheerful and self-possessed, and, to the inquiry how she had slept, replied, "Well, thanks, very well, up to four o'clock in the morning. But your Scottish carpenters seem to come to work very early. I suppose they are putting up their scaffolding quickly, though, for they are quiet now."

Her remarks were followed by a dead silence, and, to her surprise, she noticed that the faces of the family party were very pale. But, she was asked, as she valued the friendship of all there, never to speak on that subject again, there had been no carpenters at Glamis for months past. The lady, it seems, had not the remotest idea that the hammering she had heard was connected with any story, and had no notion of there being some mystery connected with the noise until enlightened on the matter at the breakfast table.

At Rushen Castle, Isle of Man, there is said to be a room which has never been opened in the memory of man. Various explanations have been assigned to account for this circumstance, one being that the old place was once inhabited by giants, who were dislodged by Merlin, and such as were not driven away remain spellbound beneath the castle. Waldron, in his "Description of the Isle of Man," has given a curious tradition respecting this strange room, in which the supernatural element holds a prominent place, and which is a good sample of other stories of the same kind: "They say there are a great many fine apartments underground, exceeding in magnificence any of the upper rooms. Several men, of more than ordinary courage have, in former times, ventured down to explore the secrets of this subterranean dwelling-place, but as none of them ever returned to give an account of what they saw, the passages to it were kept continually shut that no more might suffer by their temerity. But about fifty years since, a person of uncommon courage obtained permission to explore the dark abode. He went down, and returned by the help of a clue of packthread, and made this report: 'That after having passed through a great number of vaults he came into a long narrow place, along which having travelled, as far as he could guess, for the space of a mile, he saw a little gleam of light. Reaching at last the end of this lane of darkness, he perceived a very large and magnificent house, illuminated with a great many candles, whence proceeded the light just mentioned. After knocking at the door three times, it was opened by a servant, who asked him what he wanted. "I would go as far as I can," he replied; "be so kind as to direct me, for I see no passage but the dark cavern through which I came hither." The servant directed him to go through the house, and led him through a long entrance passage and out at the back door. After walking a considerable distance, he saw another house, more magnificent than the former, where he saw through the open windows lamps burning in every room. He was about to knock, but looking in at the window of a low parlour, he saw in the middle of the room a large table of black marble, on which lay extended a monster of at least fourteen feet long, and ten round the body, with a sword beside him. He therefore deemed it prudent to make his way back to the first house where the servant reconducted him, and informed him that if he had knocked at the second door he never would have returned. He then took his leave, and once more ascended to the light of the sun.'"

But, leaving rooms of this supernatural kind, we may allude to those which have acquired a strange notoriety from certain peculiarities of a somewhat gruesome character; and, with tales of horror attached to their guilty walls, it is not surprising that many rooms in our old country houses have long been said to be troubled with mysterious noises, and to have an uncanny aspect. Wye Coller Hall, near Colne, which was long the seat of the Cunliffes of Billington, had a room which the timid long avoided. Once a year, it is said, a spectre horseman visits this house and makes his way up the broad oaken staircase into a certain room, from whence "dreadful screams, as from a woman, are heard, which soon subside into groans." The story goes that one of the Cunliffes murdered his wife in that room, and that the spectre horseman is the ghost of the murderer, who is doomed to pay an annual visit to the house of his victim, who is said to have predicted the extinction of the family, which has literally been fulfilled. This strange visitor is always attired in the costume of the early Stuart period, and the trappings of his horse are of a most uncouth description; the evening of his arrival being generally wild and tempestuous.

At Creslow Manor House, Buckinghamshire, there is another mysterious room which, although furnished as a bedroom, is very rarely used, for it cannot be entered, even in the daytime, without trepidation and awe. According to common report, this room, which is situated in the most ancient portion of the building, is haunted by the restless spirit of a lady, long since deceased. What the antecedent history of this uncomfortable room really is no one seems to know, although it is generally agreed that in the distant past it must have been the silent witness of some tragic occurrence.

But Littlecote House, the ancient seat of the Darrells, is renowned, writes Lord Macaulay, "not more on account of its venerable architecture and furniture, than on account of a horrible and mysterious crime which was perpetrated there in the days of the Tudors." One of the bedchambers, which is said to have been the scene of a terrible murder, contains a bedstead with blue furniture, which time has made dingy and threadbare. In the bottom of one of the bed curtains is shown a strange place where a small piece has been cut out and sewn in again—a circumstance which served to identify the scene of a remarkable story, in connection with which, however, there are several discrepancies. According to one account, when Littlecote was in possession of its founders—the Darrells—a midwife of high repute dwelt in the neighbourhood, who, on returning home from a professional visit at a late hour of the night, had gone to rest only to be disturbed by one who desired to have her immediate help, little anticipating the terrible night's adventure in store for her, and which shall be told in her own words:

"As soon as she had unfastened the door, a hand was thrust in which struck down the candle, and at the same time pulled her into the road. The person who had used these abrupt means desired her to tie a handkerchief over her head and not wait for a hat, and, leading her to a stile where there was a horse saddled, with a pillion on its back, he desired her to seat herself, and then, mounting, they set off at a brisk trot. After travelling for an hour and a half, they entered a paved court, or yard, and her conductor, lifting her off her horse, led her into the house, and thus addressed her: 'You must now suffer me to put this cap and bandage over your eyes, which will allow you to breathe and speak, but not to see. Keep up your presence of mind; it will be wanted. No harm will happen to you.' Then, taking her into a chamber, he added, 'Now you are in a room with a lady in labour. Perform your office well, and you shall be amply rewarded; but if you attempt to remove the bandage from your eyes, take the reward of your rashness.'"

Shortly afterwards a male child was born, and as soon as this crisis was over the woman received a glass of wine, and was told to prepare to return home, but in the interval she contrived to cut off a small piece of the bed curtain—an act which was supposed sufficient evidence to fix the mysterious transaction as having happened at Littlecote. According to Sir Walter Scott, the bandage was first put over the woman's eyes on her leaving her own house that she might be unable to tell which way she travelled, and was only removed when she was led into the mysterious bedchamber, where, besides the lady in labour, there was a man of a "haughty and ferocious" aspect. As soon as the child was born, adds Scott, he demanded the midwife to give it him, and, hurrying across the room, threw it on the back of a fire that was blazing in the chimney, in spite of the piteous entreaties of the mother. Suspicion eventually fell on Darrell, whose house was identified by the midwife, and he was tried for murder at Salisbury, "but, by corrupting his judge, Sir John Popham, he escaped the sentence of the law, only to die a violent death by a fall from his horse." This tale of horror, it may be added, has been carefully examined, and there is little doubt but that in its main and most prominent features it is true, the bedstead with a piece of the curtain cut out identifying the spot as the scene of the tragic act.[23]

With this strange story Sir Walter Scott compares a similar one which was current at Edinburgh during his childhood. About the beginning of the eighteenth century, when "the large castles of the Scottish nobles, and even the secluded hotels, like those of the French noblesse, which they possessed in Edinburgh, were sometimes the scenes of mysterious transactions, a divine of singular sanctity was called up at midnight to pray with a person at the point of death." He was put into a sedan chair, and after being transported to a remote part of the town, he was blindfolded—an act which was enforced by a cocked pistol. After many turns and windings the chair was carried upstairs into a lodging, where his eyes were uncovered, and he was introduced into a bedroom, where he found a lady, newly delivered of an infant.

He was commanded by his attendants to say such prayers by her bedside as were suitable for a dying person. On remonstrating, and observing that her safe delivery warranted better hopes, he was sternly commanded to do as he had been ordered, and with difficulty he collected his thoughts sufficiently to perform the task imposed on him. He was then again hurried into the chair, but as they conducted him downstairs he heard the report of a pistol. He was safely conducted home, a purse of gold was found upon him, but he was warned that the least allusion to this transaction would cost him his life. He betook himself to rest, and after a deep sleep he was awakened by his servant, with the dismal news that a fire of uncommon fury had broken out in the house of ****, near the head of the Canongate, and that it was totally consumed, with the shocking addition that the daughter of the proprietor, a young lady eminent for beauty and accomplishments had perished in the flames.

The clergyman had his suspicions; he was timid; the family was of the first distinction; above all, the deed was done, and could not be amended. Time wore away, but he became unhappy at being the solitary depository of this fearful mystery, and, mentioning it to some of his brethren, the anecdote acquired a sort of publicity. The divine, however, had long been dead, and the story in some degree forgotten, when a fire broke out again on the very same spot where the house of **** had formerly stood, and which was now occupied by buildings of an inferior description. When the flames were at their height, the tumult was suddenly suspended by an unexpected apparition. A beautiful female, in a nightdress, extremely rich, but at least half a century old, appeared in the very midst of the fire, and uttered these words in her vernacular idiom: "Anes burned, twice burned; the third time I'll scare you all." The belief in this apparition was formerly so strong that on a fire breaking out and seeming to approach the fatal spot, there was a good deal of anxiety manifested lest the apparition should make good her denunciation.

But family romance contains many such tales of horror, and one told of Sir Richard Baker, surnamed "Bloody Baker," is a match even for Blue Beard's locked chamber. After spending some years abroad in consequence of a duel, he returned to his old home at Cranbrook, in Kent; he only brought with him a foreign servant, and these two lived alone. Very soon strange stories began to be whispered of unearthly shrieks having been frequently heard at nightfall to issue from his house, and of persons who were missed and never heard of again. But it never occurred to anyone to connect incidents of this kind with Sir Richard Baker, until, one day, he formed an apparent attachment to a young lady in the neighbourhood, who always wore a great number of jewels. He had often pressed her to call and see his house, and, happening to be near it, she determined to surprise him with a visit. Her companion tried to dissuade her from doing so, but she would not be turned from her purpose. They knocked at the door, but receiving no answer determined to enter. At the head of the staircase hung a parrot, which, on their passing, cried out:

"Peapot, pretty lady, be not too bold,Or your red blood will soon run cold."

And the blood of the adventurous women did "run cold" when on opening one of the room doors they found it nearly full of the bodies of murdered persons, chiefly women. And when, too, on looking out of the window they saw "Bloody Baker" and his servant bringing in the body of a lady, paralysed with fear they concealed themselves in a recess under the staircase, and, as the murderers with their ghastly burden passed by, the hand of the murdered lady hung in the baluster of the stairs, which, on Baker chopping it off with an oath, fell into the lap of one of the concealed ladies. They quickly made their escape with the dead hand, on one of the fingers of which was a ring. Reaching home, they told the story, and in proof of it displayed the ring. Families in the neighbourhood who had lost friends or relatives mysteriously were told of this "blood chamber of horrors," and it was arranged to ask Baker to a party, apparently in a friendly manner, but to have constables concealed ready to take him into custody. He accepted the invitation, and then the lady, pretending it was a dream, told him all she had seen.

"Fair lady," said he, "dreams are nothing; they are but fables."

"They may be fables," she replied, "but is this a fable?" And she produced the hand and ring, upon which the constables appeared on the scene, and took Baker into custody. The tradition adds that he was found guilty, and was burnt, notwithstanding that Queen Mary tried to save him on account of his holding the Roman Catholic religion.[24]

This tradition, of course, must not be taken too seriously; the red hand in the armorial bearings having led, it has been suggested, to the supposition of some sanguinary business in the records of the family. Among the monuments in Cranbrook Church, Kent, there is one erected to Sir Richard Baker—the gauntlet, red gloves, helmet, and spurs, having been suspended over the tomb. On one occasion, a visitor being attracted by the colour of the gloves, was accosted by an old woman, who remarked, "Aye, Miss, those are Bloody Baker's gloves; their red colour comes from the blood he shed." But the red hand is only the Ulster badge of baronetcy, and there is scarcely a family bearing it of which some tale of murder and punishment has not been told.

FOOTNOTES:

[19] Andrew's "History of Great Britain," 1794-5.

[20] Oxford, 1857.

[21] "Scenes and Legends of the Vale of Strathmore." J. Cargill Guthrie, 1875.

[22] "All the Year Round," 1880.

[23] See "Wilts Archæological Magazine," vols. i.-x.

[24] See "Notes and Queries," 1st S., I., p. 67.

CHAPTER VI.
INDELIBLE BLOOD STAINS.

"Will all great Neptune's ocean wash this blood
Clean from my hand? No; this my hand will rather
The multitudinous seas incarnardine,
Making the green one red."—MACBETH.

It was a popular suggestion in olden times that when a person had died a violent death, the blood stains could not be washed away, to which Macbeth alludes, as above, after murdering Duncan. This belief was in a great measure founded on the early tradition that the wounds of a murdered man were supposed to bleed afresh at the approach or touch of the murderer. To such an extent was this notion carried, that "by the side of the bier, if the slightest change were observable in the eyes, the mouth, feet, or hands of the corpse, the murderer was conjectured to be present, and many an innocent spectator must have suffered death. This practice forms a rich pasture in the imagination of our old writers; and their histories and ballads are laboured into pathos by dwelling on this phenomenon."[25] At Blackwell, near Darlington, the murder of one Christopher Simpson is described in a pretty local ballad known as "The Baydayle Banks Tragedy." A suspected person was committed, because when he touched the body at the inquest, "upon his handlinge and movinge, the body did bleed at the mouth, nose, and ears," and he turned out to be the murderer. Similarly Macbeth (Act III., sc. 4), speaking of the ghost, says:—

"It will have blood; they say blood will have blood;Stones have been
known to move and trees to speak,Auguries and understood relations
haveBy magot pies and choughs and rooks brought forthThe secret'st man
of blood."

Shakespeare here, in all probability, alludes to some story in which the stones covering the corpse of a murdered man were said to have moved of themselves, and so revealed the secret. In the same way, it was said that where blood had been shed, the marks could not be obliterated, but would continually reappear until justice for the crime had been obtained. On one occasion, Nathaniel Hawthorne enjoyed the hospitality of Smithells Hall,

Lancashire, and was so impressed with the well-known legend of "The Bloody Footstep" that he, in three separate instances, founded fictions upon it. In his romance of "Septimius" he gives this graphic account of what he saw: "On the threshold of one of the doors of Smithells Hall there is a bloody footstep impressed into the doorstep, and ruddy as if the bloody foot had just trodden there, and it is averred that on a certain night of the year, and at a certain hour of the night, if you go and look at the doorstep, you will see the mark wet with fresh blood. Some have pretended to say that this is but dew, but can dew redden a cambric handkerchief? And this is what the bloody footstep will surely do when the appointed night and hour come round." A local tradition says that the stone bearing the imprint of the mysterious footprint was once removed and cast into a neighbouring wood, but in a short time it had to be restored to its original position owing to the alarming noises which troubled the neighbourhood. This strange footprint is traditionally said to have been caused by George Marsh, the martyr, stamping his foot to confirm his testimony, and has been ever since shewn as the miraculous memorial of the holy man. The story is that "being provoked by the taunts and persecutions of his examiner, he stamped with his foot upon a stone, and, looking up to heaven, appealed to God for the justice of his cause, and prayed that there might remain in that place a constant memorial of the wickedness and injustice of his enemies." It is also stated that in 1732 a guest sleeping alone in the Green Chamber at Smithells Hall saw an apparition, in the dress of a minister with bands, and a book in his hand. The ghost of Marsh, for so it was pronounced to be, disappeared through the doorway, and on the owner of Smithells hearing the story, he directed that divine service—long discontinued—should be resumed at the hall chapel every Sunday.[26]

Then there are the blood stains on the floor at the outer door of the Queen's apartments in Holyrood Palace, where Rizzio was murdered. Sir Walter Scott has made these blood marks the subject of a jocular passage in his introduction to the "Chronicles of the Canongate," where a Cockney traveller is represented as trying to efface them with the patent scouring drops which it was his mission to introduce into use in Scotland. In another of his novels—"The Abbot"—Sir Walter Scott alludes to the Rizzio blood stains, and in his "Tales of a Grandfather" he deliberately states that the floor at the head of the stair still bears visible marks of the blood of the unhappy victim. In support of these blood stains, it has been urged that "the floor is very ancient, manifestly much more so than the late floor of the neighbouring gallery, which dated from the reign of Charles II. It is in all likelihood the very floor upon which Mary and her courtiers trod. The stain has been shown there since a time long antecedent to that extreme modern curiosity regarding historical matters which might have induced an imposture, for it is alluded to by the son of Evelyn as being exhibited in the year 1722."[27]

At Condover Hall, Shropshire, there is supposed to be a blood stain which has been there since the time of Henry VIII., and cannot be effaced. According to a local tradition, which has long been current in the neighbourhood, it is the blood of Lord Knevett—the owner of the hall and estate at this period—who was treacherously slain by his son. But unfortunately this piece of romance, which is utterly at variance with facts bearing on the history of Condover and its owners in years gone by, must be classed among the legendary tales of the locality. One room in Clayton Old Hall, Lancashire, has for years past been knicknamed "The Bloody Chamber," from some supposed stains of human gore on the oaken floor planks. Numerous stories have, at different times, been started to account for these blood-tokens, which have gained all the more importance from the mansion having, from time immemorial, been the favourite haunt of a mischievious boggart until laid by the parson, and now—

Whilst ivy climbs and holly is greenClayton Hall boggart shall no more be seen.

In Lincoln Cathedral there are two fine rose windows, one made by a master workman, and the other by his apprentice, out of the pieces of stained glass the former had thrown aside. The apprentice's window was declared to be the more magnificent, when the master, in a fit of chagrin, threw himself from the gallery beneath his boasted chef d'œuvre, and was killed upon the spot. But his blood-stains on the floor are declared to be indelible. At Cothele, a mansion on the banks of the Tamar, the marks are still visible of the blood spilt by the lord of the manor when, for supposed treachery, he slew the warder of the drawbridge; but these are only to be seen on a wet day.

But there is no mystery about the so-called "Bloody Chamber," for the marks are only in reality natural red tinges of the wood, denoting the presence of iron.

In addition to the appearance of such indelible marks of crime, oftentimes the ghost of the spiller of blood, or of the murdered person, haunts the scene. Thus, Northam Tower, Yorkshire, an embattled structure of the time of Henry VII.—a true Border mansion—has long been famous for the visits of some mysterious spectre in the form of a lady who was cruelly murdered in the wood, her blood being pointed out on the stairs of the old tower. Another tragic story is told of the Manor House which Bishop Pudsey built at Darlington. It was for very many years a residence of the Bishops of Durham, and a resting place of Margaret, bride of James

IV., of Scotland, and daughter of Henry VII., in her splendid progress through the country. This building was restored at great expense in the year 1668, and gained a widespread notoriety on account of the ghost story of Lady Jerratt, who was murdered there; but, as a testimony of the violent death she had received, "she left on the wall ghastly impressions of a thumb and fingers in blood for ever," and always made her appearance with one arm, the other having been cut off for the sake of a valuable ring on one of the fingers.

One room of Holland House is supposed to be haunted by Lord Holland, the first of his name and the chief builder of this splendid old mansion. According to Princess Marie Lichtenstein, in her "History of Holland House," "the gilt room is said to be tenanted by the solitary ghost of its first lord, who, runs the tradition, issues forth at midnight from behind a secret door, and walks slowly through the scenes of former triumphs with his head in his hand." And to add to this mystery, there is a tale of three spots of blood on one side of the recess whence he issues—three spots which can never be effaced.

Stains of blood—stains that cannot be washed away—are to be seen on the floor of a certain room at Calverley Hall, Yorkshire. And there is one particular flag in the cellar which is never without a mysterious damp place upon it, all the other flags being dry. Of course these are the witnesses of a terrible tragedy which was committed years ago within the walls of Calverley Hall. It appears that Walter Calverley, who had married Philippa Brooke, daughter of Lord Cobham, was a wild reckless man, though his wife was a most estimable and virtuous lady, and that one day he went into a fit of insane jealousy, or pretended to do so, over the then Vavasour of Weston. Money lenders, too, were pressing him hard, and he had become desperate. Rushing madly into the house, he plunged a dagger into one and then into another of his children, and afterwards tried to take the life of their mother, a steel corset which she wore luckily saving her life. Leaving her for dead, he mounted his horse with the intention of killing the only other child he had, and who was then at Norton. But being pursued by some villagers, his horse stumbled and threw him off, and the assassin was caught, being pressed to death at York Castle for his crimes. Not only have the stains of this bloody tragedy ever since been indelible, but the spirit of Walter Calverley could not rest, having often been seen galloping about the district at night on a headless horse.[28] And, speaking of ghosts which appear in this eccentric fashion, we may note that Eastbury House, near Blandford—now pulled down—had in a certain marble-floored room, ineffaceable stains of blood, attributable, it is said, to the suicide of William Doggett, the steward of Lord Melcombe, whose headless spirit long haunted the neighbourhood.

As a punishment for her unnatural cruelty in causing her child's death, it is commonly reported that the spirit of Lady Russell is doomed to haunt Bisham Abbey, Berkshire, the house where this act of violence was committed. Lady Russell had by her first husband a son, who, unlike herself, had a natural antipathy to every kind of learning, and so great was his obstinate repugnance to learning to write that he would wilfully blot over his copy-books in the most careless and slovenly manner. This conduct so irritated his mother that, to cure him of the propensity, she beat him again and again severely, till at last she beat him to death. To atone for her cruelty, she is now doomed to haunt the room where the fatal deed was perpetrated; and, as her apparition glides along, she is always seen in the act of washing the blood stains of her son from her hands. Although ever trying to free herself of these marks of her unnatural crime, it is in vain, as they are indelible stains which no water will remove.

By a strange coincidence, some years ago, in altering a window shutter, a quantity of antique copy-books were discovered pushed into the rubble between the joints of the floor, and one of these books was so covered with blots as to fully answer the description in the narrative above. It is noteworthy, also, that Lady Russell had no comfort in her sons by her first husband. Her youngest son, a posthumous child, caused her special trouble, insomuch so that she wrote to her brother-in-law, Lord Burleigh, for advice how to treat him. This may have been, it has been suggested, the unfortunate boy who was flogged to death, though he seems to have lived to near man's estate. Lady Russell was buried at Bisham, by the remains of her first husband, Sir Thomas Hoby, and her portrait may still be seen, representing her in widow's weeds and with a very pale face.

A mysterious crime is traditionally reported to have, some years ago, taken place at the old parsonage at Market, or East Lavington, near Devizes—now pulled down. The ghost of the lady supposed to have been murdered haunted the locality, and it has been said a child came to an untimely end in the house. "Previous to the year 1818," writes a correspondent of Notes and Queries, "a witness states his father occupied the house, and writes that 'in that year on Feast Day, being left alone in the house, I went to my room. It was the one with marks of blood on the floor. I distinctly saw a white figure glide into the room. It went round by the washstand near the bed and disappeared!'" It may be added that part of the road leading from Market Lavington to Easterton which skirts the grounds of Fiddington House, used to be looked upon as haunted by a lady who was locally known as the "Easterton ghost." But in the year 1869 a wall was built round the roadside of the pond, and curiously close to the spot where the lady had been in the habit of appearing two skeletons were disturbed—one of a woman, the other of a child. The bones were buried in the churchyard, and no ghost, it is said, has since been seen. It would seem, also, that blood stains, wherever they may fall, are equally indelible; and even to this day the New Forest peasant believes that the marl he digs is still red with the blood of his ancient foes, the Danes, a form of superstition which we find existing in various places.

For very many years the road from Reigate to Dorking, leading through a lonely lane into the village of Buckland, was haunted by a local spectre known as the "Buckland Shag," generally supposed to have been connected with a love tragedy. In the most lonely part of this lane a stream of clear water ran by the side of—which laid for years—a large stone, concerning which the following story is told: Once on a time, a lovely blue-eyed girl, whose father was a substantial yeoman in the neighbourhood, was wooed and won by the subtle arts of an opulent owner of the Manor House of Buckland.

In the silence of the evening this lane was their accustomed walk, the scene of her devoted love and of his deceitful vows. Here he swore eternal fidelity, and the unsuspecting girl trusted him with the confiding affection of her innocent heart. It was at such a moment that the wily seducer communicated to her the real nature of his designs, the moon above being only the witness of his perfidy and her distress. She heard the avowal in tremulous silence, but her deadly paleness, and her expressive look of mingled reproach and terror created alarm even in the mind of her would-be seducer, and he hastily endeavoured to recall the fatal declaration; but it was too late, she sprang from his agitated grasp, and, with a sigh of agony, fell dead at his feet.

When he beheld the work of his iniquitous designs, he was seized with distraction, and drawing a dagger from his bosom, he plunged it into his own false heart, and lay stretched by the side of her he had so basely wronged. On the morrow, as a peasant passed over the little stream, he saw a dark stone with drops of blood trickling from its heart into the pure limpid water. From that day the stream retained its untainted purity, and the stone continued its sacrifice of blood.

Soon afterwards a terrific object was seen hovering at midnight about this fatal spot, taking its position at first upon the "bleeding stone," but it was ousted by the lord of the manor, who removed the blood-tainted stone to his own premises, to satisfy the timid minds of his neighbours. But the stone still continued to bleed, nor did its removal in any way intimidate the spectre. Connected with this alarming midnight visitor, writes a correspondent of The Gentleman's Magazine, "I remember a circumstance related to me by those who were actually acquainted with the facts, and with the person to whom they refer. An inhabitant of Buckland, who had attended Reigate Market and become exceedingly intoxicated, was joked by a companion upon the subject of the 'Buckland Shag,' whereupon he laid a wager that if Shag appeared in his path that night he would fight him with his trusty hawthorn. Accordingly he set forth, and arrived at the haunted spot. The spectre stood in his path, and, raising his stick, he struck it with all his strength, but it made no impression, nor did the goblin move. The stick fell as upon a blanket—so the man described it—and he instantly became sober, while a cold tremor ran through every nerve of his athletic frame.

He hurried on, and the spectre followed. At length he arrived at his own door; then, and not till then, did the spectre vanish, leaving the affrighted man in a state of complete exhaustion upon the threshold of his cottage. He was carried to his bed, and from that bed he never rose again; he died in a week."

Similarly, there is a romantic old legend connected with Kilburn Priory, to the effect that there was formerly, not far distant, a stone of dark red colour, which was said to be the stain of the blood of St. Gervase de Mertoun. The story goes that Stephen de Mertoun, being enamoured of his brother's wife, made immoral overtures to her, which she threatened to make known to Sir Gervase, to prevent which disclosure Stephen resolved to waylay his brother and slay him. By a strange coincidence, the identical stone on which his murdered body had expired formed a part of his tomb, and the eye of the murderer resting upon it, adds the legend, blood was seen to issue from it. Struck with horror at this sight, Stephen de Mertoun hastened to the Bishop of London, and making confession of his guilt, demised his property to the Priory of Kilburn.

In the same way the Cornishman knows, from the red, filmy growth on the brook pebbles, that blood has been shed—a popular belief still firmly credited. Some years ago a Cornish gentleman was cruelly murdered, and his body thrown into a brook; but ever since that day the stones in this brook are said to be spotted with gore—a phenomenon which had never occurred previously. And, according to another strange Cornish belief told of St. Denis's blood, it is related that at the very time when his decapitation took place in Paris, blood fell on the churchyard of St. Denis. It is further said that these blood stains are specially visible when a calamity of any kind is near at hand; and before the breaking out of the plague, it is said the stains of the blood of St. Denis were seen; and, "during our wars with the Dutch, the defeat of the English fleet was foretold by the rain of gore in this remote and sequestered place."

It is also a common notion that not only are the stains of human blood wrongfully shed ineffaceable, but a curse lights upon the ground, causing it to remain barren for ever. There is, for instance, a dark-looking piece of ground devoid of verdure in the parish of Kirdford, Sussex. Local tradition says that this was formerly green, but the grass withered gradually away soon after the blood of a poacher, who was shot there, trickled down on the place. But perhaps the most romantic tale of this kind was that known as the "Field of Forty Footsteps." A legendary story of the period of the Duke of Monmouth's Rebellion describes a mortal conflict which took place between two brothers in Long Fields, afterwards called Southampton Fields, in the rear of Montague House, Bloomsbury, on account of a lady who sat by. The combatants fought so furiously as to kill each other, after which their footsteps, imprinted on the ground in the vengeful struggle, were reported "to remain, with the indentations produced by their advancing and receding; nor would any grass or vegetation grow afterwards over these forty footsteps." The most commonly received version of the story is, that two brothers were in love with the same lady, who would not declare a preference for either, but coolly sat upon a bank to witness the termination of a duel which proved fatal to both. Southey records this strange story in his "Commonplace Book,"[29] and after quoting a letter from a friend, recommending him to "take a view of those wonderful marks of the Lord's hatred to duelling, called 'The Brothers' Steps,'" he thus describes his own visit to the spot: "We sought for near half an hour in vain. We could find no steps at all within a quarter of a mile, no, nor half a mile, of Montague House. We were almost out of hope, when an honest man, who was at work, directed us to the next ground adjoining to a pond. There we found what we sought, about three-quarters of a mile north of Montague House and five hundred yards east of Tottenham Court Road. The steps are of the size of a large human foot, about three inches deep, and lie nearly from north-east to south-west. We counted only twenty-six; but we were not exact in counting. The place where one or both the brothers are supposed to have fallen is still bare of grass. The labourer also showed us the bank where, the tradition is, the wretched woman sat to see the combat." Miss Porter and her sister founded upon this tragic romance their story, "Coming Out, or the Field of Forty Footsteps"; and at Tottenham Street Theatre was produced, many years ago, an effective melodrama based upon the same incident, entitled "The Field of Footsteps."

Another romantic tale of a similar nature is connected with Montgomery Church walls, and is locally designated "The Legend of the Robber's Grave," of which there are several versions, the most popular one being this: Once upon a time, a man was said to have been wrongfully hanged at Montgomery; and, when the rope was round his neck, he declared in proof of his innocence that grass would never grow on his grave. Curious to relate, be the cause what it may, there is yet to be seen a strip of sterility—in the form of a cross—amidst a mass of verdure.[30]

Likewise, the peasantry still talk mysteriously of Lord Derwentwater's execution, and tell how his blood could not be washed away. Deep and lasting were the horror and grief which were felt when the news of his death reached his home in the north. The inhabitants of the neighbourhood, it is said, saw the coming vengeance of heaven in the Aurora Borealis which appeared in unwonted brilliancy on the evening of the execution, and which is still known as "Lord Derwentwater's Light" in the northern counties; the rushing Devil's Water, too, they said, ran down with blood on that terrible night, and the very corn which was ground on that day came tinged from the mill with crimson. Lord Derwentwater's death, too, was all the more deplored on account of his having long been undecided as to whether he should embrace the enterprise against the House of Hanover. But there had long been a tradition in his family that a mysterious and unearthly visitant appeared to the head of the house in critical emergencies, either to warn of danger, or to announce impending calamity. One evening, a few days before he resolved to cast in his lot with the Stuarts, whilst he was wandering amid the solitudes of the hills, a figure stood before him in robe and hood of grey.

This personage is said to have sadly reproached the Earl for not having already joined the rising, and to have presented him with a crucifix which was to render him secure against bullet or sword thrust. After communicating this message the figure vanished, leaving the Earl in a state of bewilderment. The mysterious apparition is reported to have spoken with the voice of a woman, and as it is known that "in the more critical conjunctures of the history of the Stuarts every device was practised by secret agents to gain the support of a wavering follower," it is not difficult to guess at a probable explanation of the ghost of the Dilston Groves. It may be added that at Dilston, Lady Derwentwater was long said to revisit the pale glimpses of the moon to expiate the restless ambition which impelled her to drive Lord Derwentwater to the scaffold.

But how diverse have been the causes of many of these romantic blood stains may be gathered from another legendary tale connected with Plaish Hall, near Cardington, Shropshire. The report goes that a party of clergymen met together one night at Plaish Hall to play cards. In order that the real object of their gathering might not be known to any but themselves, the doors were locked. Before very long, however, they flew open without any apparent cause. Again they were locked, but presently they burst open a second time, and even a third. Astonished at what seemed to baffle explanation, and whilst mutually wondering what it could mean, a panic was suddenly created when, in their midst, there appeared a mysterious figure resembling the Evil One. In a moment the invited guests all rose and fled, leaving the unfortunate host by himself "face to face with the enemy."

What happened after their departure was never divulged, for no one "ever saw that wretched man again, either alive or dead." That he had died some violent death was generally surmised, for a great stain of blood shaped like a human form was found on the floor of the room, and despite all efforts the mark could never be washed out. Ever since this inexplicable occurrence, the house has been haunted, and at midnight a ghostly troop of horses are occasionally heard, creating so much noise as to awaken even heavy sleepers.

And Aubrey in his "Miscellanies" tells how when the bust of Charles I., carved by Bernini, "was brought in a boat upon the Thames, a strange bird—the like whereof the bargemen had never seen—dropped a drop of blood, or blood-like, upon it, which left a stain not to be wiped off." The strange story of this ill-fated bust is more minutely told by Dr. Zacharay Grey in a pamphlet on the character of Charles I.: "Vandyke having drawn the king in three different faces—a profile, three-quarters, and a full face—the picture was sent to Rome for Bernini to make a bust from it. Bernini was unaccountably dilatory in the work, and upon this being complained of, he said that he had set about it several times, but there was something so unfortunate in the features of the face that he was shocked every time that he examined it, and forced to leave off the work, and, if there was any stress to be laid on physiognomy, he was sure the person whom the picture represented was destined to a violent end."

The bust was at last finished and sent to England. As soon as the ship that brought it arrived in the river, the king, who was very impatient to see the bust, ordered it to be carried immediately to Chelsea. It was conveyed thither, and placed upon a table in the garden, whither the king went with a train of nobility to inspect the bust. As they were viewing it, a hawk flew over their heads with a partridge in his claws, which he had wounded to death. Some of the partridge's blood fell upon the neck of the bust, where it remained without being wiped off. This bust was placed over the door of the king's closet at Whitehall and continued there till the palace was destroyed by fire.

FOOTNOTES:

[25] D'Israeli's "Curiosities of Literature."

[26] See Harland and Wilkinson's "Lancashire Folklore," 135-136.

[27] "Book of Days," I., 235.

[28] This tradition is the basis of the drama called "The Yorkshire Tragedy," and was adopted by Ainsworth in his "Romance of Rookwood."

[29] 2nd Ser., p. 21.

[30] A curious legend is related by Roger de Hoveden, which shows the antiquity of the Wakefield mills. "In the year 1201, Eustace, Abbot of Flaye, came over into England, preaching the duty of extending the Sabbath from three o'clock p.m. on Saturday to sunrising on Monday morning, pleading the authority of an epistle written by Christ himself, and found on the altar of St. Simon at Golgotha. The people of Yorkshire treated the fanatic with contempt, and the miller of Wakefield persisted in grinding his corn after the hour of cessation, for which disobedience his corn was turned into blood, while the mill-wheel stood immovable against all the water of the Calder."

CHAPTER VII.
CURIOUS SECRETS.

"And now I will unclasp a secret book,
And to your quick-conceiving discontent
I'll read your matter deep and dangerous."

1. HENRY IV., Act 1., sc. 3.

"The Depository of the Secrets of all the World" was the inscription over one of the brazen portals of Fakreddin's valley, reminding us of what Ossian said to Oscar, when he resigned to him the command of the morrow's battle, "Be thine the secret hill to-night," referring to the Gaelic custom of the commander of an army retiring to a secret hill the night before a battle to hold communion with the ghosts of departed heroes. But, as it has been often remarked of secrets—both political and social—they are only too frequently made to be revealed, a truth illustrative of Ben Jonson's words in "The Case is Unaltered "—

A secret in his mouthIs like a wild bird put into a cage,Whose door no sooner opens but 'tis out.

In family history, some of the strangest secrets have related to concealment of birth, many a fraud having been devised to alter or perpetuate the line of issue. Early in the present century, a romantic story which was the subject of conversation in the circles both of London and Paris, related to Lady Newborough, who had always considered herself the daughter of Lorenzo Chiappini, formerly gaoler of Modigliana, and subsequently constable at Florence, and of his wife Vincenzia Diligenti. Possessed in her girlhood of fascinating appearance and charming manners, she came out as a ballet dancer at the principal opera at Florence, and one night she so impressed Lord Newborough that, by means of a golden bribe, he had her transferred from the stage to his residence. His conduct towards her was tender and affectionate, and, in spite of the disparity of years, he afterwards married her, introducing her to the London world as Lady Newborough.

Some time after her marriage, according to a memoir stated to be written by the fair claimant of the House of Orleans, and printed in Paris before the Revolution of 1830 but immediately suppressed, when staying at Sienna she received a posthumous letter from her supposed father, which, from its extraordinary disclosures, threw her into complete bewilderment.[31] It ran as follows:

MY LADY,—I have at length reached the term of my days without having revealed to anyone a secret which directly concerns me and yourself. The secret is this:

On the day when you were born, of a person whom I cannot name and who now is in the other world, a male child of mine was also born. I was requested to make an exchange; and, considering the state of my finances in those days, I accepted to the often-repeated and advantageous proposals, and at that time I adopted you as my daughter in the same manner as my son was adopted by the other party.

I observe that heaven has repaired my faults by placing you in better circumstances than your father, although his rank was somewhat similar. This enables me to end my days with some comfort.

Let this serve to extenuate my culpability towards you. I entreat your pardon for my fault. I desire you, if you please, to keep this transaction secret, in order that the world shall not have any opportunity to speak of an affair which is now without remedy.

This, my letter, you will not receive until after my death.

LORENZO CHIAPPINI.

After receiving this letter, Lady Newborough sent for Ringrezzi, the confessor of the late gaoler, and Fabroni, a confessor of the late Countess Borghi, and was told by the former that, in his opinion, she was the daughter of the Grand Duke Leopold; but the latter disagreed, saying, "Myladi is the daughter of a French lord called Count Joinville, who had considerable property in Champagne; and I entertain no doubt that if your ladyship were to go to that province you would there find valuable documents, which I have been told were there left in the hands of a respectable ecclesiastic."

It is further stated that two old sisters of the name of Bandini, who had been born and educated in the house of the Borghis, and been during all their life in the service of that family, informed Lady Newborough, and afterwards in the Ecclesiastical Court of Faenza, that in the year 1773 they followed their master and mistress to Modigliana, where the latter usually had their summer residence in a chateau belonging to them; that, arriving there, they found a French count, Louis Joinville, and his countess, established in the Pretorial Palace. They further affirmed that between the

Borghis and this family a very intimate intercourse was soon established and that they daily interchanged visits.

Furthermore, the foreign lord, it is said, was extremely familiar with persons of the lowest rank, and particularly with the gaoler, Chiappini, who lived under the same roof. The wives of both were pregnant; and it appeared that they expected their delivery much about the same time. But the Count was tormented with a grievous anxiety; his wife had as yet had no male offspring, and he much feared that they would never be blessed with any. Having communicated his project to the Borghis, he at length made an overture to the gaoler, telling him he apprehended the loss of a very great inheritance, which absolutely depended on the birth of a son, and that he was disposed, in case the Countess gave birth to a daughter, to exchange her for a boy, and that for this exchange he would liberally recompense the father. The man, highly pleased at finding his fortune thus unexpectedly made, immediately accepted the offer, and the bargain was concluded.

Immediately after the accouchment of the ladies, one of the Bandinis went to the Pretorial Palace to see the new-born babies, when some women in the house told her that the exchange had already taken place; and Chappiani himself being present, confirmed their statement. But as there were several persons in the secret—however solemnly secrecy had been promised—public rumour soon accused the barterers. The Count Louis, fearing the people's indignation, concealed himself in the Convent of St. Bernard, at Brisighella.

The lady, it is added, departed with her supposititious son; her own daughter being baptized and called Maria Stella Petronilla, and designated as the daughter of Lorenzo Chappiani and Vincenzia Diligenti.

Having learnt so much, Lady Newborough being in Paris in the year 1823, had recourse to a stratagem by which she expected to gain additional information. Accordingly she inserted in the newspapers, "that she had been desired by the Countess Pompeo Borghi to discover in France a Count Louis Joinville, who in the year 1773 was with his Countess at Modigliana, where the latter gave birth to a son on the 16th April, and that if either of these persons were still alive, or the child born at Modigliana, she was empowered to communicate to them something of the highest importance.

Subsequently to this advertisement, she was waited upon by a Colonel Joinville, but he derived his title only from Louis XVIII. But before the Colonel was out of the door, she had a call from the Abbé de Saint-Fare, whom she gave to understand that she was anxious to discover the identity of a birth connected with the sojourn with the late Comte de Joinville. In the course of conversation, this Abbé is stated to have made most injudicious admissions, from which Lady Newborough gathered that he was the confidential agent of the Duke of Orleans, being currently said to be his illegitimate brother.

Lady Newborough was now convinced in her own mind that she was the eldest child of the late Duke of Orleans, and hence was the first princess of the blood of France, and the rightful heiress of immense wealth. But this discovery brought her no happiness, and subjected to her to much discomfort and misery. Her story—whether true or false—will in all probability remain a mystery to the end of time, being one of those political puzzles which must remain an open question.

Secret intrigue, however, at one time or another, has devised the most subtle plans for supplanting the rightful owner out of his birthright—a second wife through jealously entering into some shameful compact to defraud her husband's child by his former wife of his property in favour of her own. Such a secret conspiracy is connected with Draycot, and, although it has been said to be one of the most mysterious in the whole range of English legends, yet, singular as the story may be, writes Sir Bernard Burke, "no small portion of it is upon record as a thing not to be questioned; and it is not necessary to believe in supernatural agency to give all parties credit for having faithfully narrated their impressions." The main facts of this strange story are briefly told: Walter Long of Draycot had two wives, the second being Catherine, daughter of Sir John Thynne, of Longleat. On their arrival at Draycot after the honeymoon, there were great rejoicings into which all entered save the heir of the houses of Draycot and Wraxhall, who was silent and sad. Once arrived in her new home, the mistress of Draycot lost no time in studying the character of her step-son, for she had an object in view which made it necessary that she should completely understand his character. Her design was, in short, that the young master of Draycot, "the heir of all his father's property—the obstruction in the way of whatever children there might be by the second marriage—must be ruined, or at any rate so disgraced as to provoke his father to disinherit him." Taking into her confidence her brother, Sir Egremont Thynne, of Longleat, with his help she soon discovered that the youthful heir of Draycot was fond of wine and dice, and that he had on more than one occasion met with his father's displeasure for indulgence in such acts of dissipation. Having learnt, too, that the young man was kept on short supplies by his parsimonious father, and had often complained that he was not allowed sufficient pocket-money for the bare expenses of his daily life; the crafty step-mother seized this opportunity for carrying out her treacherous and dishonourable conduct. Commiserating with the inexperienced youth in his want of money, and making him feel more than ever dissatisfied at his father's meanness to him, she quickly enlisted him on her side, especially when she gave him liberal supplies of money, and recommended him to enjoy his life whilst it was in his power to do so.

With a full rather than an empty purse, the young squire was soon seen with a cheerful party over the wine bottle, and, at another time, with a gambling group gathered round the dice box. But this kind of thing suited admirably his step-mother, for she took good care that such excesses were brought under the notice of the lad's father, and magnified into heinous crimes. From time to time this unprincipled woman kept supplying the unsuspecting youth with money, and did all in her power to encourage him in his tastes for reckless living. Fresh stories of his son's dissipated conduct were continually being told to the master of Draycot, until at last, "influenced by the wiles of his charming wife, on the other by deeper wiles of his brother-in-law, he agreed to make out a will disinheriting his son by his first wife, and settling all his possessions on his second wife and her relations."

Hitherto, the secret entered into by brother and sister had been a perfect success, for not only was the son completely alienated from his father, but the latter deemed it a sin to make any provision for one who was given to drink and gambling. A draft will was drawn up by Sir Egremont Thynne, and when approved of was ordered to be copied by a clerk. But here comes the remarkable part of the tale. The work of engrossing demands a clear, bright light, and the slightest shadow intervening between the light and the parchment would be sure to interrupt operations. Such an interruption the clerk was suddenly? subjected to, when, "on looking up he beheld a white hand—a lady's delicate white hand—so placed between the light and the deed as to obscure the spot on which he was engaged. The unaccountable hand, however, was gone almost as soon as noticed." The clerk concluding that this was some optical delusion, proceeded with his work, and had come to the clause wherein the Master of Draycot disinherited his son, when again the same ghostly hand was thrust between the light and the parchment.

Terrified at this unearthly intervention, the clerk awoke Sir Egremont from his midnight slumbers, and told him what had occurred, adding that the spectre hand was no other than that of the first wife of the master of Draycot, who resented the cruel wrong done to her son. In due time the deed was engrossed by another clerk, and duly signed and sealed.

But the "white hand" had not appeared in vain, for the clerk's curious adventure afterwards became the topic of general conversation, and the injustice done to the disinherited heir of Draycot excited so much sympathetic indignation that "the trustees of the late Lady Long arrested the old knight's corpse at the church door, her nearest relations commenced a suit against the intended heir, and the result was a compromise between the parties, John Long taking possession of Wroxhall, while his other half-brother was allowed to retain Draycot," a settlement that, it is said, explains the division of the two estates, which we find at the present day. The secret between the brother and sister was well kept, and whatever explanation may be given to the "white hand," the story is as singular as any in the annals of domestic history.

It was the betrayal of a secret, on the other hand, on the part of a woman that is traditionally said to have caused the sudden and tragic death of Richard, second Earl of Scarborough. This nobleman, it seems, was in the confidence of the King, and had been entrusted by him with the keeping of a most important secret. But, like most favourites, the Earl was surrounded by enemies who were ever on the alert to compass his ruin, and, amidst other devices, they laid their plans to prevail on the unsuspecting Earl to betray the confidence which the King had implicitly reposed on him. Finding it, however, impossible by this means to make him guilty of a breach of trust towards the King, they had recourse to another scheme which proved successful, and thereby irrevocably compromised him in the King's eyes.

Having discovered that the Earl was in love with a certain lady and was in the habit of frequently visiting her, some of his enemies discovered where she lived, and, calling on her, promised an exceeding rich reward if she could draw the royal secret from her lover, and communicate it to them. Easily bought over by the offer of so rich a bribe, the treacherous woman, like Delilah of old, soon prevailed upon the Earl to give her the desired information, and the secret was revealed. As soon as the Earl's enemies were apprised of the same, they lost no time in hurrying to the king, and submitting to him the proofs of his protégé's imprudence. They gained their end, for the next time the Earl came into the royal presence, the King said to him in a sad but firm voice, "Lumley, you have lost a friend, and I a good servant." This was a bitter shock to the Earl, for he learnt now for the first time that she in whom he had reposed his love and faith had been his worst enemy, and that, as far as his relations to the King were concerned, he was disgraced as a man of honour in his estimation. With his proud and haughty spirit, unable to bear the misery and chagrin of his fall and ruin, he had recourse to the suicide's escape from trouble—he shot himself.

But another secret, no less tragic and of a far more sensational nature, related to a certain Mr. Macfarlane. One Sunday, in the autumn of the year 1719, Sir John Swinton, of Swinton, in Berwickshire, left his little daughter Margaret, who had been indisposed through a childish ailment, at home when he went with the rest of his family to church, taking care to lock the outer door. After the lapse of an hour or so, the child had become dull through being alone, and she made her way into the parlour below stairs, where, on her arrival, she hastily bolted the door to keep out any ghost or bogie, stories relating to which had oftentimes excited her fears. But great was her terror when, on looking round, she was confronted by a tall lady, gracefully attired, and possessed of remarkable handsome features. The poor child stood motionless with terror, afraid to go forwards or backwards. Her throbbing heart, however, quickly recovered from its fright, as the mysterious lady, with a kind eye and sweet smile, addressed her by name, and taking her hand, spoke:

"Margaret, you may tell your mother what you have seen, but, for your life, to no one else. If you do, much evil may come of it, some of which will fall on yourself. You are young, but you must promise to be silent as the grave itself in this matter."

Full of childish wonderment, Margaret, half in shyness and half in fear at being an agent in so strange a secret, turned her head towards the window, but on turning round found the lady had disappeared, although the door remained bolted. Her curiosity was now more than before aroused, and she concluded that after all this lady must be one of those fairies she had often read of in books; and it was whilst pondering on what she had seen that the family returned from church.

Surprised at finding Margaret bolted in this parlour, Sir John learnt that "she had been frightened, she knew not why, at the solitude of her own room, and had bolted herself in the parlour." Although she was soon laughed out of her childish fears, Lady Swinton was quick enough to perceive that Margaret had not communicated everything, and insisted upon knowing the whole truth. The child made no objection, as she had not been told to keep the secret from her mother. After describing all that happened, Lady Swinton kissed her daughter tenderly and said, "Since you have kept the secret so well, you shall know something more of this strange lady."

Thereupon Lady Swinton pushed aside one of the oaken panels in the parlour, which revealed a small room beyond, where sat the mysterious lady. "And now, Margaret dear," said her mother, "listen to me. This lady is persecuted by cruel men, who, if they find her, will certainly take her life. She is my guest, she is now yours, and I am sure I need not tell you the meanest peasant in all Scotland would shame to betray his guest."

Margaret promised to keep the secret, never evincing the slightest curiosity to know who the lady was, and it is said she had reached her twentieth year when one day the adventure of her childhood was explained.

It seems that the lady in question was a Mrs. Macfarlane, daughter of Colonel Charles Straiton, a zealous Jacobite. When about nineteen years old she married John Macfarlane—law agent of Simon Fraser, Lord Lovat—who was many years her senior. Soon after her marriage Mrs. Macfarlane made the acquaintance of Captain John Cayley, a commissioner of Customs, and on September 29th, 1716, he called on her at Edinburgh, when, for reasons only known to herself or him, she fired two shots at him with a pistol, one of which pierced his heart.

According to Sir Bernard Burke, it was when she would not yield to Captain Cayley's immoral overtures that the latter vowed to blacken her character, a threat which he so successfully carried out "that not one of her female acquaintances upon whom she called would admit her; not one of all she met in the street would acknowledge her." Desperate at this villainy on his part, Mrs. Macfarlane, under pretence of agreeing to Captain Cayley's overtures, sent for him, when fully confident that he was about to reap the fruit of his infamous daring he obeyed her summons. But no sooner had he entered the room than she locked the door, and, snatching up a brace of pistols, she exclaimed: "Wretch, you have blasted the reputation of a woman who never did you the slightest wrong. You have fixed an indelible stain upon the child at her bosom; and all this because, coward as you are, you thought there was no one to take her part." At the same time, it is said, she fired two shots at him with a pistol, one of which pierced his heart. Her husband asserted, however, that she fired to save herself from outrage, an explanation which she affirmed was "only too true." Her husband also declared that his wife was desirous of sending for a magistrate and of telling him the whole story, but that he advised her against it. But not appearing to stand her trial in the ensuing February, she was outlawed, and obtained refuge in the mansion house of the Swinton family in the concealed apartment already described.[32] According to Sir Walter Scott, she "returned and lived and died in Edinbugh"; but her life must have been comparatively short, as her husband married again on October 6th, 1719.

Akin to this dramatic episode may be mentioned one concerning Robert Perceval, the second son of the Right Hon. Sir John Perceval, when reading for the law in his chambers in Lincoln's Inn. The clock had just struck the hour of midnight, when, on looking up from his book, he was astonished to see a figure standing between himself and the door, completely muffled up in a long cloak so as to defy recognition.

"Who are you?" But the figure made no answer.

"What do you want?" No reply.

The figure stood motionless. Thinking it made a low hollow laugh, the young student struck at the intruder with his sword, but the weapon met with no resistance, and not a single drop of blood stained it.

This was amazing, and still no answer. Determined to solve the mystery of this strange being, he cast aside its cloak, when lo! "he saw his own apparition, bloody and ghostly, whereat he was so astonished that he immediately swooned away, but, recovering, he saw the spectre depart."

At first this occurrence left the most unpleasant impressions on his mind, but as days passed by without anything happening, the warning, or whatever it was, faded gradually from his memory, and he lived as before, drinking and quarrelling, managing to embroil himself at play with the celebrated Beau Fielding. The day at last came, however, when his equanimity was disturbed, for, as he was walking from his chambers in Lincoln's Inn to a favourite tavern in the Strand, he imagined that he was followed by an ungainly looking man. He tried to avoid him, but the man followed on, and after a time, fully convinced that he was dogged by this man, he demanded "Who he was, and why he followed him?"

"THE FIGURE STOOD MOTIONLESS.

But the man replied, "I am not following you; I'm following my own business."

By no means satisfied, young Perceval crossed over to the opposite side of the street, but the man followed him step by step, and before many minutes had elapsed he was joined by another man as ungainly-looking as himself. Perceval, no longer doubting that he was followed, called upon the two men to retire at their peril, and although he succeeded in making them take to their heels after a sharp sword skirmish, he was himself wounded in the leg, and made his way to the nearest tavern. This unpleasant encounter, reviving the memory of the ghastly figure he had seen in his chambers, made him feel that he was a doomed man, and he was not far wrong, for that night near the so-called May-pole in the Strand he was found dead—but how he died was a secret never divulged.

Another equally strange incident connected with this mysterious crime happened to a Mrs. Brown, "perhaps from her holding some situation in the family of his uncle, Sir Robert." On this fatal night, writes Sir Bernard Burke, she dreamt that one Mrs. Shearman—the housekeeper—came to her and asked for a sheet.

She demanded, "for what purpose," to which Mrs. Shearman replied, "Poor Master Robert is killed, and it is to wind him in."

Curious to say, in the morning Mrs. Shearman came at an early hour into her room, and asked for a sheet. For what purpose? inquired Mrs Brown.

"Poor Mr. Robert is murdered," was the reply; "he lies dead in the Strand watch-house, and it is to wind his body in."

In the year 1848, the Warwick magistrates investigated a most extraordinary and preposterous charge of murder against Lord Leigh, his deceased mother, and persons employed by them, in the course of which inquiry one of the accusers professed to have been in possession of a secret connected with the matter for a number of years. The accusation seems to have originated from the attempt of certain parties to seize Stoneleigh Abbey on pretence that it rightfully belonged to them, and not to Lord Leigh. In November, 1844, a mob took possession of the place for one George Leigh; several of the ringleaders were tried for the offence, and not fewer than twenty-eight were convicted. The account of this curious conspiracy, as given in the "Annual Register," goes on to say that Richard Barnett made the charge of murder: in 1814 he was employed under Lady Julia Leigh and her son at the Abbey, where a number of workmen were engaged in making alterations; four of these men were murdered by large stones having been allowed to fall on them, and their bodies were placed within an abutment of a bridge, and then inclosed with masonry. Another man was shot by Hay, a keeper. In cross-examination, the witness said he "had kept silence on these atrocities for thirty years, because he feared Lord Leigh, and because he did not expect to obtain anything by speaking. He first divulged the secret to those who were trying to seize the estate; as this information he thought would help them to get it, for the murders were committed to keep out the proper owners."

In the course of the inquiry, John Wilcox was required to repeat evidence which he had given before a Master of Chancery; but, instead of doing so, the man confessed that he was not sober when he made the declaration. He further declared how some servants of the Leigh family had burned pictures, and had been paid to keep "the secrets of the house." The whole story, however, was a deliberate and wilful fabrication, the facts were contradicted and circumstantially refuted, and of course so worthless a charge was dismissed by the Bench.

FOOTNOTES:

[31] See "Annual Register" (1832), 152-5.

[32] This incident suggested to Sir Walter Scott his description of the concealment and discovery of the Countess of Derby in "Peveril of the Peak." See "Dictionary of National Biography," xxxv., 74.

CHAPTER VIII.
THE DEAD HAND.

> Open, lock,
> To the dead man's knock!
> Fly, bolt, and bar, and band;
> Nor move, nor swerve,
> Joint, muscle, or nerve,
> At the spell of the dead man's hand.
>
> INGOLDSBY LEGENDS.

One of the most curious and widespread instances of deception and credulity is the magic potency which has long been supposed to reside in the so-called "Hand of Glory"—the withered hand of a dead man. Numerous stories are told of its marvellous properties as a charm, and on the Continent many a wonderful cure is said to have been wrought by its agency. Southey, it may be remembered, in his "Thalaba, the Destroyer," has placed it in the hands of the enchanter, King Mohareb, when he would lull to sleep Zohak, the giant keeper of the Caves of Babylon. And the history of this wonder-working talisman, as used by Mohareb, is thus graphically told:

Thus he said,And from his wallet drew a human hand,Shrivelled and dry and black.And fitting, as he spake,A taper in his hold,Pursued: "A murderer on the stake had died.I drove the vulture from his limbs and loptThe hand that did the murder, and drew upThe tendon strings to close its grasp,And in the sun and windParched it, nine weeks exposed."

From the many accounts given of this "Dead Hand," we gather that it has generally been considered necessary that the hand should be taken from a man who has been put to death for some crime. Then, when dried and prepared with certain weird unguents, it is ready for use. Sir Walter Scott, in the "Antiquary" has introduced this object of superstition, making the German adventurer, Dousterswivel, describe it to the assembled party among the ruins at St. Ruth's thus jocosely: "De Hand of Glory is very well known in de countries where your worthy progenitors did live; and it is a hand cut off from a dead man as he has been hanged for murder, and dried very nice in de smoke of juniper wood; then you do take something of de fatsh of de bear, and of de badger, and of de great eber (as you do call ye grand boar), and of de little sucking child as has not been christened (for dat is very essential), and you do make a candle, and put into de Hand of Glory at de proper hour and minute, with the proper ceremonials; and he who seeketh for treasures shall never find none at all."

Possessed of these mystic qualities, such a hand could not fail to find favour with those engaged in any kind of evil and enterprise; and, on account of its lulling to sleep all persons within the circle of its influence, was of course held invaluable by thieves and burglars. Thus the case is recorded of some thieves, who, a few years ago, attempted to commit a robbery on a certain estate in the county Meath. To quote a contemporary account of the affair, it appears that "they entered the house armed with a dead man's hand, with a lighted candle in it, believing in the superstitious notion that a candle placed in a dead man's hand will not be seen by any but by those by whom it is used, and also that if a candle in a dead hand be introduced into a house, it will prevent those who may be asleep from awaking. The inmates, however, were alarmed, and the robbers fled, leaving the hand behind them." Another story communicated by the Rev. S. Baring-Gould, tells how two thieves, having come to lodge in a public-house, with a view to robbing it, asked permission to pass the night by the fire, and obtained it. But when the house was quiet the servant girl, suspecting mischief, crept downstairs, and looked through the keyhole. She saw the men open a sack, and take out a dry withered hand. They anointed the fingers with some unguents, and lighted them. Each finger flamed, but the thumb they could not light—that was because one of the household was not asleep.

The girl hastened to her master, but found it impossible to arouse him—she tried every other sleeper, but could not break the charmed sleep. At last stealing down into the kitchen, while the thieves were busy over her master's strong-box, she secured the hand, blew out the flames, and at once the whole house was aroused.

Among other qualities which have been supposed to belong to a dead man's hand, are its medicinal virtues, in connection with which may be mentioned the famous "dead hand," which was, in years past, kept at Bryn Hall, Lancashire. There are several stories relating to this gruesome relic, one being that it was the hand of Father Arrowsmith, a priest, who, according to some accounts, is said to have been put to death for his religion in the time of William III. It is recorded that when about to suffer he desired his spiritual attendant to cut off his right hand, which should ever after have power to work miraculous cures on those who had faith to believe in its efficacy. This relic, which forms the subject of one of Roby's "Traditions of Lancashire," was preserved with great care in a white silk bag, and was resorted to by many diseased persons, who are reported to have derived wonderful cures from its application. Thus the case is related of a woman who, attacked with the smallpox, had this dead hand in bed with her every night for six weeks, and of a poor lad living near Manchester who was touched with it for the cure of scrofulous sores.

It has been denied, however, that Father Arrowsmith was hanged for "witnessing a good confession," and Mr. Roby, in his "Traditions of Lancashire," says that, having been found guilty of a rape, in all probability this story of his martyrdom, and of the miraculous attestation to the truth of the cause for which he suffered, were contrived for the purpose of preventing the scandal that would have come upon the Church through the delinquency of an unworthy member. It is further said that one of the family of the Kenyons attended as under-sheriff at the execution, and that he refused the culprit some trifling favour at the gallows, whereupon Arrowsmith denounced a curse upon him, to wit, that, whilst the family could boast of an heir, so long they never should want a cripple—a prediction which was supposed by the credulous to have been literally fulfilled. But this story is discredited, the real facts of the case, no doubt, being that he was hanged "under sanction of an atrocious law, for no other reason but because he had taken orders as a Roman Catholic priest, and had endeavoured to prevail upon others to be of his own faith." According to another version of the story, Edmund Arrowsmith was a native of Haydock, in the parish of Winwick. He entered the Roman Catholic College of Douay, where he was educated, afterwards being ordained priest. But in the year 1628 he was apprehended and brought to Lancaster on the charge of being a priest contrary to the laws of the realm, and was executed on 26th August, 1628, his last words being "Bone Jesu."[33] As recently as the year 1736, a boy of twelve years, the son of Caryl Hawarden, of Appleton-within-Widnes, county of Lancaster, is stated to have been cured of what appeared to be a fatal malady by the application of Father Arrowsmith's hand, which was effected in the following manner: The boy had been ill fifteen months, and was at length deprived of the use of his limbs, with loss of his memory and impaired sight. In this condition, which the physicians had declared hopeless, it was suggested to his parents that, as wonderful cures had been effected by the hand of "the martyred saint," it was advisable to try its effects upon their afflicted child. The "holy hand" was accordingly procured from Bryn, packed in a box and wrapped in linen. Mrs. Hawarden, having explained to the invalid boy her hopes and intentions, applied the back part of the dead hand to his back, stroking it down each side the backbone and making the sign of the Cross, which she accompanied with a fervent prayer that Jesus Christ would aid it with His blessing. Having twice repeated this operation, the patient, who had before been utterly helpless, rose from his seat and walked about the house, to the surprise of seven persons who had witnessed the miracle. From that day the boy's pains left him, his memory was restored, and his health became re-established. This mystic hand, it seems, was removed from Bryn Hall to Garswood, a seat of the Gerard family, and subsequently to the priest's house at Ashton-in-Makerfield. But many ludicrous tales are current in the neighbourhood, of pilgrims having been rather roughly handled by some of the servants, such as getting a good beating with a wooden hand, so that the patients rapidly retraced their steps without having had the application of the "holy hand."

It is curious to find that such a ghastly relic as a dead hand should have been preserved in many a country house, and used as a talisman, to which we find an amusing and laughable reference in the "Ingoldsby Legends":

Open, lock,To the dead man's knock!Fly bolt, and bar, and band;Nor move, nor swerve,Joint, muscle, or nerve,At the spell of the dead man's hand.Sleep, all who sleep! Wake, all who wake!But be as dead for the dead man's sake.

The story goes on to tell how, influenced by the mysterious spell of the enchanted hand, neither lock, bolt, nor bar avails, neither "stout oak panel, thick studded with nails"; but, heavy and harsh, the hinges creak, though they had been oiled in the course of the week, and

The door opens wide as wide may be,And there they stand,That wondrous band,Lit by the light of the glorious hand,By one! by two! by three!

At Danesfield, Berkshire—so-called from an ancient horseshoe entrenchment of great extent near the house, supposed to be of Danish origin—is preserved a withered hand, which has long had the reputation of being that presented by Henry I. to Reading Abbey, and reverenced there as the hand of James the Apostle. It answers exactly to "the incorrupt hand" described by Hoveden, and was found among the ruins of the abbey, where it is thought to have been secreted at the dissolution.

FOOTNOTES:

[33] Baines's "Lancashire," iii., 638; Harland and Wilkinson's "Lancashire Folklore," 158-163.

CHAPTER IX.
DEVIL COMPACTS.

MEPHISTOPHELES.—I will bind myself to your service here, and never sleep nor slumber at your call. When we meet on the other side, you shall do as much for me.

GOETHE'S "Faust."

The well-known story of Faust reminds us of the many similar weird tales which have long held a prominent place in family traditions. But in the majority of cases the devil is cheated out of his bargain by some spell against which his influence is powerless. According to the popular notion, compacts are frequently made with the devil, by which he is bound to complete, for instance, a building—as a house, a church, a bridge, or the like—within a certain period; but, through some artifice, by which the soul of the person for whom he is doing the work is saved, the completion of the undertaking is prevented: Thus the cock is made to crow, because, like all spirits that shun the light of the sun, the devil loses his power at break of day. The idea of bartering the soul for temporary gain has not been confined to any country, but as an article of terrible superstition has been widespread. Mr Lecky has pointed out how, in the fourteenth century, "the bas-reliefs on cathedrals frequently represent men kneeling down before the devil, and devoting themselves to him as his servants." In our own country, such compacts were generally made at midnight in some lonely churchyard, or amid the ruins of some castle. But fortunately for mankind, by resorting to spells and counterspells the binding effects of these "devil-bonds" as they have been termed were, in most cases, rendered ineffectual, the devil thereby losing the advantage.

It is noteworthy that the wisdom of the serpent is frequently outwitted by a crafty woman, or a cunning priest. A well-known Lancashire tradition gives a humorous account of how the devil was on one occasion deluded by the shrewdness of a clever woman. Barely three miles from Clitheroe, on the high road to Gisburne, stood a public house with this title, "The Dule upo' Dun," which means "The Devil upon Dun" (horse). The story runs that a poor tailor sold himself to Satan for seven years on his granting him certain wishes, after which term, according to the contract, signed, as is customary, with the victim's own blood, his soul was to become "the devil's own." When the fatal day arrived, on the advice of his wife, he consulted "the holy father of Salley" in his extremity. At last the hour came when the Evil One claimed his victim, who tremblingly contended that the contract was won from him by fraud and dishonest pretences, and had not been fulfilled. He even ventured to hint at his lack of power to bestow riches, or any great gift, on which Satan was goaded into granting him another wish. "Then," said the trembling tailor, "I wish thou wert riding back again to thy quarters on yonder dun horse, and never able to plague me again, or any other poor wretch whom thou has gotten into thy clutches!"

The words were no sooner uttered than the devil, with a roar which was heard as far as Colne, went away rivetted to the back of this dun horse, the tailor watching his departure almost beside himself for joy. He lived for many years in health and affluence, and, at his death, one of his relatives having bought the house where he resided, turned it into an inn, having for his sign, "The Dule upo' Dun." On it was depicted "Old Hornie" mounted on a scraggy dun horse, without saddle or bridle, "the terrified steed being off and away at full gallop from the door, while a small hilarious tailor with shears and measures," viewed his departure with anything but grief or disapprobation.[34] The authors of "Lancashire Legends," describing this old house, inform us that it was "one of those ancient gabled black and white edifices, now fast disappearing under the march of improvement. Many windows of little lozenge-shaped panes set in lead, might be seen here in all the various stages of renovation and decay. Over the door, till lately, swung the old and quaint sign, attesting the truth of the tradition."

Occasionally similar bargains have been rendered ineffectual by cunning device. In the north wall of the church of Tremeirchion, North Wales, has long been shown the tomb of a former vicar, who was also celebrated as a necromancer, flourishing in the middle of the fourteenth century. It is reported that he proved himself more clever than the Wicked One himself. A bargain was made between them that the vicar should practise the black art with impunity during his life, but that the devil should possess his body after death, whether he were buried within or without the church. But the worthy vicar dexterously cheated his ally of his bargain by being buried within the church wall itself. A similar tradition is told of other localities, and amongst them of Barn Hall, in the parish of Tolleshunt Knights, on the border of the Essex marshes. In the middle of a field is shown an enclosed uncultivated spot, where, the legend says, it was originally intended to erect the hall, had not the devil come by night and destroyed the work of the day. This kind of thing went on for some time, when it was arranged that a knight, attended by two dogs, should watch for the author of this mischief. He had not long to wait, for, in the quiet of the night, the Prince of Darkness made his appearance, bent on his mischievous errand. A tussle ensued, in the course of which, snatching up a beam from the building, he hurled it to the site of the present hall, exclaiming:

"Wheresoe'er this beam shall fall,There shall stand Barn Hall."

But the devil, very angry at being thus foiled by the knight, vowed that he would have him at his death, whether he was buried in the church or out of it. "But this doom was averted by burying him in the wall—half in and half out of the church. At Brent Pelham Church, Herts, too, there is the tomb of one Piers Shonkes, and there is a tale current in the neighbourhood that the devil swore he would have him, no matter whether buried within or without the church. So, as a means of escape, he was built up in the wall of the sacred edifice."

Another extraordinary story has long been told of Hermitage Castle, one of the most famous of the Border Keeps in the days of its splendour. It is not surprising, therefore, that for many years past it has had the reputation of being haunted, having been described as:—

"Haunted Hermitage,Where long by spells mysterious bound,They pace their round with lifeless smile,And shake with restless foot the guilty pile,Till sink the smouldering towers beneath the burdened ground."

It is popularly said that Lord Soulis, "the evil hero of Hermitage," in an unguarded moment made a compact with the devil, who appeared to him in the shape of a spirit wearing a red cap, which gained its hue from the blood of human victims in which it was steeped. Lord Soulis sold himself to the demon, and in return he was permitted to summon his familiar, whenever he was desirous of doing so, by rapping thrice on an iron chest, the condition being that he never looked in the direction of the spirit. But one day, whether wittingly or not has never been ascertained, he failed to comply with this stipulation, and his doom was sealed. But even then the foul fiend kept the letter of the compact. Lord Soulis was protected by an unholy charm against any injury from rope or steel; hence cords could not bind him, and steel could not slay him. But when at last he was delivered over to his enemies, it was found necessary to adopt the ingenious and effective expedient of rolling him up in a sheet of lead, and boiling him to death, and so:

On a circle of stones they placed the pot,On a circle of stones but barely nine;They heated it red and fiery hotAnd the burnished brass did glimmer and shine.They rolled him up in a sheet of lead—A sheet of lead for a funeral pall;They plunged him into the cauldron redAnd melted him, body, lead, bones and all.

This was the terrible end of the body of Lord Soulis, but his spirit is supposed to still linger on the scene. And once every seven years he keeps tryst with Red Cap on the scene of his former devilries.

And still when seven years are o'erIs heard the jarring soundWhen hollow opes the charmèd doorOf chamber underground.

A tradition well-known in Yorkshire relates how on the Eagle's Crag, otherwise nicknamed the "Witches' Horseblock," the Lady of Bernshaw Tower made that strange compact with the devil, whereby she not only became mistress of the country around, but the dreaded queen of the Lancashire witches. It seems that this Lady Sybil was possessed of almost unrivalled beauty, and scarcely a day passed without some fresh admirer seeking her hand—an additional attraction being her great wealth. Her intellectual attainments, too, were commonly said to be far beyond those of her sex, and oftentimes she would visit the Eagle's Crag in order to study nature and admire the varied aspects of the surrounding country.

LADY SYBIL AT THE EAGLES' CRAG.

It was on these occasions that Lady Sybil often felt a strong desire to possess supernatural powers; and, in an unwary moment, it is said that she was induced to sell her soul to the devil, in order that she might be able to take a part in the nightly revelries of the then famous Lancashire witches. It is added that the bond was duly attested with her blood, and that in consequence of this compact her utmost wishes were at all times granted. Hapton Tower was, at this time, occupied by a junior branch of the Towneley family, and, although Lord William had long been a suitor for the hand of Lady Sybil, his proposals were constantly rejected. In his despair, he determined to consult a famous Lancashire witch—one Mother Helston—who promised him success on the ensuing All Hallows' Eve. When the day arrived, in accordance with her directions, he went out hunting, and on nearing Eagle's Crag he started a milk-white doe, but, after scouring the country for miles—the hounds being well-nigh exhausted—he returned to the Crag. At this crisis, a strange hound joined them—the familiar of Mother Helston, which had been sent to capture Lady Sibyl, who had assumed the disguise of the white doe. The remainder of the curious family legend, as told by Mr. Harland, is briefly this: During the night, Hapton Tower was shaken as by an earthquake, and in the morning the captured doe appeared as the fair heiress of Bernshaw. Counter spells were adopted, her powers of witchcraft were suspended, and before many days had passed Lord William had the happiness to lead his newly-wedded bride to his ancestral home. But within a year she had renewed her diabolical practices, causing a serious breach between her husband and herself. Happily a reconciliation was eventually effected, but her bodily strength gave way, and her health rapidly declined. When it became evident that the hour of her death was drawing near, Lord William obtained the services of the neighbouring clergy, and by their holy offices the devil's bond was cancelled. Soon afterwards, Lady Sybil died in peace, but Bernshaw Tower was from that time deserted. Popular tradition, however, still alleges that her grave was dug where the dark Eagle's Crag shoots out its cold, bare peak into the sky, and on the eve of All Hallows, the hound and the milk-white doe are supposed by the peasantry to meet on the Crag, pursued by a spectre huntsman in full chase. It is further added that the belated peasant crosses himself at the sound, remembering the sad fate of Lady Sybil of Bernshaw Tower.

It is curious to find no less a person than Sir Francis Drake charged with having been befriended by the devil; and the many marvellous stories current respecting him still linger among the Devonshire peasantry. By the aid of the devil, it is said, he was enabled to destroy the Spanish Armada. And his connection with the old Abbey of Buckland is equally singular. An extensive building attached to the abbey, for instance, which was no doubt used as barns and stables after the place had been deprived of its religious character, was reported to have been built by the devil in three nights. "After the first night," writes Mr. Hunt,[35] "the butler, astonished at the work done, resolved to watch and see how it was performed. Consequently, on the second night, he mounted into a large tree and hid himself between the forks of its five branches. At midnight, so the story goes, the devil came, driving teams of oxen, and, as some of them were lazy, he plucked this tree from the ground and used it as a goad. The poor butler lost his senses and never recovered them." Although, as it has been truly remarked, "on the waters that wash the shores of the county of Devon were achieved many of those triumphs which make Sir Francis Drake's life read more like a romance than a sober chronicle of facts;" the extraordinary traditions told respecting him have largely invested his life with the supernatural. But, whatever may have been the nature of his dealings with the devil, we are told that he has had to pay dearly for any earthly advantages he may have derived therefrom in his lifetime, "being forced to drive at night a black hearse, drawn by headless horses, and urged on by running devils and yelping headless dogs, along the road from Tavisk to Plymouth."

Among the many tales related, in which the demoniacal element holds a prominent place, there is one relating to the projected marriage of his wife. It seems that Sir Francis was abroad, and his wife, not hearing from him for seven years, concluded he must be dead, and hence was at liberty to enter for a second time the holy estate of matrimony. Her choice was made and the nuptial day fixed; but Sir Francis Drake was informed of all this by a spirit that attended him. And just as the wedding was about to be solemnised, he hastily charged one of his big guns and discharged a ball. So true was the aim that "the ball shot up right through the globe, dashed through the roof of the church, and fell with a loud explosion between the lady and her intended bridegroom." The spectators and assembled guests were thrown into the wildest confusion; but the bride declared it was an indication that Sir Francis Drake was still alive, and, as she refused to allow another golden circlet to be placed on her finger, the intended ceremony was, in the most abrupt and unexpected manner, ended. The prettiest part of the tale remains to be told. Not long afterwards Sir Francis Drake returned, and, disguised as a beggar, he solicited alms from his wife at her own door; when, unable to prevent smiling in the midst of a feigned tale of abject poverty, she recognised him, and a very joyful meeting took place.

And even Buckland Abbey did not escape certain strange influences. Some years ago, a small box was found in a closet which had been long closed, containing, it is supposed, family papers. It was arranged that this box should be sent to the residence of the inheritor of the property. The carriage was at the abbey door, into which it was easily lifted. The owner having taken his seat, the coachman attempted to start his horses, but in vain. They would not, they could not, move. More horses were brought and then the heavy farm horses, and eventually all the oxen. They were powerless to start the carriage. At length a mysterious voice was heard declaring that the box could never be moved from Buckland Abbey. Accordingly it was taken from the carriage easily by one man, and a pair of horses galloped off with the carriage.

The famous Jewish banker, Samuel Bernard, who died in the year 1789, leaving an enormous property, had, it is said, "a favourite black cock which was regarded by many as uncanny, and as unpleasantly connected with the amassing of his fortune." The bird died a day or two before his master. It would seem that in bygone years black cocks were extensively used in magical incantations and in sacrifices to the devil, and Burns, it may be remembered, in his "Address to the Deil" says, "Some cock or cat your rage must stop;" and a well-known French recipe for invoking the Evil One runs thus: "Take a black cock under your left arm, and go at midnight to where four cross roads meet. Then cry three times 'Poul Noir!' or else utter 'Robert' nine times, and the devil will appear."

Among the romantic stories told of Kersal Hall, Lancashire, it is related how Eustace Dauntesey, one of its chiefs in days of old, wooed a maiden fair with a handsome fortune; but she gave her heart to a rival suitor. The wedding day was fixed, but the prospect of her marriage was a terrible trouble to Eustace, and threatened to mar the happiness of his life. Having, however, in his youth perfected himself in the black art, he drew a magic circle, at the witching hour of night, and summoned the Evil One to a consultation. The meeting came off, at which the usual bargain was quickly struck, the soul of Eustace being bartered for the coveted body of the beautiful young lady. The compact, it was arranged, should close at her death, but the Evil One was to remain meanwhile by the side of Dauntesey in the form of an elegant "self," or genteel companion. In due course the eventful day arrived when Eustace stood before the altar. But the marriage ceremony was no sooner over than, on leaving the sacred edifice, the elements were found to be the reverse of favourable to them. The flowers strewed before their feet stuck to their wet shoes, and soaking rain cast a highly depressing influence on all the bridal surroundings; and, on arriving at the festive hall where the marriage feast was to be held, the ill-fortune of Eustace assumed another shape. Strange to say, his bride began to melt away before his very eyes, and, thoroughly familiar as he was with the laws of magic, here was a new phase of mystery which was completely beyond his comprehension. In short, poor Eustace was the wretched victim of a complete swindle, for while, on the one hand, something is recorded about "a holy prayer, a sunny beam, and an angel train bearing the fair maiden slowly to a fleecy cloud, in whose bosom she became lost to earth," Dauntesey, on the other hand, awakened to consciousness by a touch from his sinister companion, saw a huge yawning gulf at his feet, and felt himself gradually sinking in a direction exactly the opposite of that taken by his bride, who, in the short space of an hour, was lost to him for ever.

But one of the most curious cases of this kind was that recorded in an old tractate[36] published in 1662, giving an account attested by "six of the sufficientest men of the town," of what happened to a certain John Leech, a farmer living at Raveley. Being desirous of visiting Whittlesea fair, he went beforehand with a neighbour to an inn for the purpose of drinking "his morninges draught." Whilst the two were enjoying their "morninges draught," Mr. Leech began to be "very merry," and, seeing his friend was desirous of going, he exclaimed, "Let the devil take him who goeth out of this house to-day." But in his merriment he forgot his rash observation, and shortly afterwards, calling for his horse, set out for the fair. He had not travelled far on the road when he remembered what he had said, "his conscience being sore troubled at that damnable oath which he had took." Not knowing what to do, he rode about, first one way and then another, until darkness set in, and at about two o'clock in the night "he espied two grim creatures before him in the likeness of griffins." These were the devil's messengers, who had been sent to take him at his word, and take him they did, according to the testimony of the "six sufficientist men of the town." They roughly handled him, took him up in the air, stripped him, and then dropped him, "a sad spectacle, all bloody and goared," in a farmyard just outside the town of Doddington.

Here he was discovered, lying upon some harrows, in the condition described. He was picked up, and carried to a gentleman's house, where, being well cared for, he narrated the remarkable adventure which had befallen him. Before long, however, he "grew into a frenzy so desperate that they were afraid to stay in his chamber," and the gentleman of the house, not knowing what to do, "sent for the parson of the town." Prompted, it is supposed, by the Satanic influence which still held him, Mr. Leech rushed at the minister, and attacked him with so much fury that it was "like to have cost him his life." But the noise being heard below, the servants rushed up, rescued the parson, and tied Mr. Leech down in his bed, and left him. The next morning, hearing nothing, they thought he was asleep, but on entering his room "he was discovered with his neck broke, his tongue out of his mouth, and his body as black as a shoe, all swelled, and every bone in his body out of joint."[37]

We may conclude these extraordinary cases of "devil-bonds" with two further strange incidents, one an apparent record of a case of a similar kind, which was practised, amidst the frivolities and plotting of the French Court, by no less celebrated a lady than Catharine de Medicis. In the "Secret History of France for the Last Century,"[38] this incredible story is given: "In the first Civil War, when the Prince of Conde was, in all appearance, likely to prevail, and Katherine was thought to be very near the end of her much desired Regency, during the young king's minority, she was known to have been for two days together retired to her closet, without admitting her menial servants to her presence." Some few days after, having called for Monsieur de Mesme, one of the Long Robe, and always firm to her interest, she delivered him a steel box, fast locked, to whom she said, giving him the key: 'That in respect she knew not what might come to her by fortune, amidst those intestine broils that then shook France, she had thought fit to enclose a thing of great value within that box, which she consigned to his care, not to open it upon oath, but by an express order under her own hand.' The queen dying without ever calling for the box, it continued many years unopened in the family of De Mesme, after both their deaths, till, at last, curiosity, or the suspicion of some treasure, from the heaviness of it, tempted Monsieur de Mesme's successor to break it open, which he did. Instead of any rich present from so great a queen, what horror must the lookers on have when they found a copper plate of the form and bigness of one of the ancient Roman Votive Shields, on which was engraved Queen Katherine de Medicis on her knees, in a praying posture, offering up to the devil sitting upon a throne, in one of the ugliest shapes they used to paint him, Charles the IXth, then reigning, the Duke of Anjou, afterwards Henry III., and the Duke of Alanson, her three sons, with this motto in French, "So be it, I but reign."And in the Court Rolls of the Manor of Hatfield, near the Isle of Axholme, Yorkshire, the following ridiculous story is given: "Robert de Roderham appeared against John de Ithon, for that he had not kept the agreement made between them, and therefore complains that on a certain day and year, at Thorne, there was an agreement between the aforesaid Robert and John, whereby the said John sold to the said Robert the Devil, bound in a certain bond, for threepence farthing, and thereupon, the said Robert delivered to the said John one farthing as earnest money, by which the property of the said devil, was vested in the person of the said Robert, to have livery of the said devil on the fourth day next following, at which day the said Robert came to the forenamed John and asked delivery of the said devil, according to the agreement between them made. But the said John refused to deliver the said devil, nor has he yet done it, &c., to the great damage of the said Robert, to the amount of 60gs, and he has, therefore, brought his suit."The said John came, and did not deny the said agreement; and because it appeared to the Court that such a suit ought not to subsist among Christians, the aforesaid parties are, therefore, adjourned to the infernal regions, there to hear their judgment, and both parties were amerced by William de Scargell, Seneschall."

FOOTNOTES:

[34] Harland and Wilkinson's "Lancashire Legends," 15-16.

[35] "Romances of the West of England."

[36] "A Strange and True Relation of one Mr. John Leech," 1662.

[37] "Saunders' Legends and Traditions of Huntingdonshire," 1878, 1-3.

[38] London, printed for A. Bell, 1714.

CHAPTER X.
FAMILY DEATH OMENS.

"Say not 'tis vain! I tell thee, some
Are warned by a meteor's light,
Or a pale bird flitting calls them home,
Or a voice on the winds by night—
And they must go. And he too, he,
Woe for the fall of the glorious tree."

—MRS. HEMANS.

A curious chapter in the history of many of our old county families is that relating to certain forewarnings, which, from time immemorial, have been supposed to indicate the approach of death. However incredible the existence of these may seem, their appearance is still intimately associated with certain houses, instances of which have been recorded from time to time. Thus Cuckfield Place, Sussex, is not only interesting as a fine Elizabethan mansion, but as having suggested to Ainsworth the "Rookwood Hall" of his striking romance. "The supernatural occurrence," he says, "forming the groundwork of one of the ballads which I have made the harbinger of doom to the house of Rookwood, is ascribed, by popular superstition, to a family resident in Sussex, upon whose estate the fatal tree—a gigantic lime, with mighty arms and huge girth of trunk—is still carefully preserved." In the avenue that winds towards the house the doom-tree still stands:—

"And whether gale or calm prevail, or threatening cloud hath fled,By hand of Fate, predestinate, a limb that tree will shed;A verdant bough, untouched, I trow, by axe or tempest's breath,To Rookwood's head, an omen dread of fast approaching death."

"Cuckfield Place," adds Ainsworth, "to which this singular piece of timber is attached, is the real Rookwood Hall, for I have not drawn upon imagination, but upon memory, in describing the seat and domains of that fated family." A similar tradition is associated with the Edgewell Oak, which is said to indicate the coming death of an inmate of Castle Dalhousie by the fall of one of its branches; and Camden in his "Magna Britannia," alluding to the antiquity of the Brereton family, relates this peculiar fact which is reported to have been repeated many times: "This wonderful thing respecting them is commonly believed, and I have heard it myself affirmed by many, that for some days before the death of the heir of the family the trunk of a tree has always been seen floating in the lake adjoining their mansion;" a popular superstition to which Mrs. Hemans refers in the lines which head the present chapter. A further instance of a similar kind is given by Sir Bernard Burke, who informs us that opposite the dining-room at Gordon Castle is a large and massive willow tree, the history of which is somewhat singular. Duke Alexander, when four years old, planted this willow in a tub filled with earth. The tub floated about in a marshy-piece of land, till the shrub, expanding, burst its cerements, and struck root in the earth below; here it grew and prospered till it attained its present goodly size. It is said the Duke regarded the tree with a sort of fatherly and even superstitious regard, half-believing there was some mysterious affinity between its fortune and his own. If an accident happened to the one by storm or lightning, some misfortune was not long in befalling the other.

It has been noted, also, that the same thing is related of the brave but unfortunate Admiral Kempenfeldt, who went down in the Royal George off Portsmouth. During his proprietary of Lady Place, he and his brother planted two thorn trees. But one day, on coming home, the brother noted that the tree planted by the Admiral had completely withered away. Astonished at this unexpected sight, he felt some apprehensions as to Admiral Kempenfeldt's safety, and exclaimed with some emotion, "I feel sure that this is an omen that my brother is dead." By a striking coincidence, his worst fears were realised, for on that evening came the terrible news of the loss of the Royal George.

Whenever any member of the family of Kirkpatrick of Closeburn, in the county of Dumfries was about to die—either by accident or disease—a swan that was never seen but on such occasions, was sure to make its appearance upon the lake which surrounded Closeburn Castle, coming no one knew whence, and passing away as mysteriously when the predicted death had taken place, in connection with which the following singular legend has been handed down: In days gone by, the lake of Closeburn Castle was the favourite resort during the summer season of a pair of swans, their arrival always being welcome to the family at the castle from a long established belief that they were ominous of good fortune to the Kirkpatricks. "No matter," it is said, "what mischance might have before impended, it was sure to cease at their coming, and so suddenly, as well as constantly, that it required no very ardent superstition to connect the two events into cause and effect."

But a century and a half had passed away, when it happened that the young heir of Closeburn Castle—a lad of not quite thirteen years of age—

in one of his visits to Edinburgh attended at the theatre a performance of "The Merchant of Venice," in the course of which he was surprised to hear Portia say of Bassanio that he should

"Make a swan-like end,Fading in music."

Often wondering whether swans really sang before dying he determined, at the first opportunity, to test the truth of these words for himself. On his return home, he was one day walking by the lake when the swans came sailing majestically towards him, and at once reminded of Portia's remark. Without a moment's thought, he lodged in the breast of the foremost one a bolt from his crossbow, killing it instantly. Frightened at what he had done, he made up his mind it should not be known; and, as the water drifted the dead body of the bird towards the shore, he buried it deep in the ground.

No small surprise, however, was occasioned in the neighbourhood, when, for several years, no swans made their annual appearance, the idea at last being that they must have died in their native home, wherever that might chance to be. The yearly visit of the swans of Closeburn had become a thing of the past, when one day much excitement was caused by the return of a single swan, and much more so when a deep blood-red stain was observed upon its breast. As might be expected, this unlooked-for occurrence occasioned grave suspicions even amongst those who had no great faith in omens; and that such fears were not groundless was soon abundantly clear, for in less than a week the lord of Closeburn Castle died suddenly. Thereupon the swan vanished, and was seen no more for some years, when it again appeared to announce the loss of one of the house by shipwreck.

The last recorded appearance of the bird was at the third nuptials of Sir Thomas Kirkpatrick, the first baronet of that name. On the wedding-day, his son Roger was walking by the lake, when, on a sudden, as if it had emerged from the waters, the swan appeared with the bleeding breast. Roger had heard of this mysterious swan, and, although his father's wedding bells were ringing merrily, he himself returned to the castle a sorrowful man, for he felt convinced that some evil was hanging over him. Despite his father's jest at what he considered groundless superstition on his part, the young man could not shake off his fears, replying to his father, "Perhaps before long you also may be sorrowful." On the night of that very day the son died, and here ends the strange story of the swans of Closeburn.[39]

Similarly, whenever two owls are seen perched on the family mansion of the noble family of Arundel of Wardour, it has long been regarded as a certain indication that one of its members before very long will be summoned out of the world; and the appearance of a white-breasted bird was the death-warning of the Oxenham family, particulars relating to the tragic origin of which are to be found in a local ballad, which commences thus[40]:

Where lofty hills in grandeur meet,And Taw meandering flows,There is a sylvan, calm retreat,Where erst a mansion rose.

There dwelt Sir James of Oxenham,A brave and generous lord;Benighted travellers never cameUnwelcome to his board.

In early life his wife had died;A son he ne'er had known;And Margaret, his age's pride,Was heir to him alone.

In course of time, Margaret became affianced to a young knight, and their wedding-day was fixed. On the evening preceding it, her father, in accordance with custom, gave a banquet to his friends, in order that they might congratulate him on the approaching happy union. He stood up to thank them for their kind wishes, and in alluding to the young knight—in a few hours time to be his daughter's husband—he jestingly called him his son:—

But while the dear unpractised wordStill lingered on his tongue,He saw a silvery breasted birdFly o'er the festive throng.

Swift as the lightning's flashes fleet,And lose their brilliant light,Sir James sank back upon his seatPale and entranced with fright.

With some difficulty he managed to conceal the cause of his embarrassment, but on the following day the priest had scarcely begun the marriage service,

When Margaret with terrific screamsMade all with horror start.Good heavens! her blood in torrents streams,A dagger in her heart.

The deed had been done by a discarded lover, who, by the aid of a clever disguise, had managed to station himself just behind her:—

"Now marry me, proud maid," he cried,"Thy blood with mine shall wed";He dashed the dagger in his side,And at her feet fell dead.

And this pathetic ballad concludes by telling us how

Poor Margaret, too, grows cold with death,And round her hovering fliesThe phantom bird for her last breath,To bear it to the skies.

Equally strange is the omen with which the ancient baronet's family of Clifton, of Clifton Hall, in Nottinghamshire, is forewarned when death is about to visit one of its members. It appears that in this case the omen takes the shape of a sturgeon, which is seen forcing itself up the river Trent, on whose bank the mansion of the Clifton family is situated. And, it may be remembered, how in the park of Chartley, near Lichfield, there has long been preserved the breed of the indigenous Staffordshire cow, of white sand colour, with black ears, muzzle, and tips at the hoofs. In the year of the battle of Burton Bridge a black calf was born; and the downfall of the great house of Ferrers happening at the same period, gave rise to the tradition, which to this day has been current in the neighbourhood, that the birth of a parti-coloured calf from the wild breed in Chartley Park is a sure omen of death within the same year to a member of the family.

By a noticeable coincidence, a calf of this description has been born whenever a death has happened in the family of late years. The decease of the Earl and his Countess, of his son Lord Tamworth, of his daughter Mrs. William Joliffe, as well as the deaths of the son and heir of the eighth Earl and his daughter Lady Frances Shirley, were each preceded by the ominous birth of a calf. In the spring of the year 1835, an animal perfectly black, was calved by one of this mysterious tribe in the park of Chartley, and it was soon followed by the death of the Countess.[41] The park of Chartley, where this weird announcement of one of the family's death has oftentimes caused so much alarm, is a wild romantic spot, and was in days of old attached to the Royal Forest of Needwood and the Honour of Tutbury—of the whole of which the ancient family of Ferrers were the puissant lords. Their immense possessions, now forming part of the Duchy of Lancaster, were forfeited by the attainder of Earl Ferrers after his defeat at Burton Bridge, where he led the rebellious Barons against Henry III. The Chartley estate, being settled in dower, was alone reserved, and has been handed down to its present possessor. Of Chartley Castle itself—which appears to have been in ruins for many years—many interesting historical facts are recorded. Thus it is said Queen Elizabeth visited her favourite, the Earl of Essex, here in August, 1575, and was entertained by him in a half-timbered house which formerly stood near the Castle, but was long since destroyed by fire. It is questionable whether Mary Queen of Scots was imprisoned in this house, or in a portion of the old Castle. Certain, however, it is that the unfortunate queen was brought to Chartley from Tutbury on Christmas day, 1585. The exact date at which she left Chartley is uncertain, but it appears she was removed thence under a plea of taking the air without the bounds of the Castle. She was then conducted by daily stages from the house of one gentleman to another, under pretence of doing her honour, without her having the slightest idea of her destination, until she found herself on the 20th of September, within the fatal walls of Fotheringhay Castle.

Cortachy Castle, the seat of the Earl of Airlie, has for many years past been famous for its mysterious drummer, for whenever the sound of his drum is heard it is regarded as the sure indication of the approaching death of a member of the Ogilvie family. There is a tragic origin given to this curious phenomenon, the story generally told being to the effect that either the drummer, or some officer whose emissary he was, had excited the jealousy of a former Lord Airlie, and that he was in consequence of this occurrence put to death by being thrust into his own drum, and flung from the window of the tower, in which is situated the chamber where his music is apparently chiefly heard. It is also said that the drummer threatened to haunt the family if his life were taken, a promise which he has not forgotten to fulfil.

Then there is the well-known tradition that prior to the death of any of the lords of Roslin, Roslin Chapel appears to be on fire, a weird occurrence which forms the subject of Harold's song in the "Lay of the Last Ministrel."

O'er Roslin all that dreary nightA wondrous blaze was seen to gleam;'Twas broader than the watch-fire lightAnd redder than the bright moonbeam.

It glared on Roslin's castled rock,It ruddied all the copse-wood glen;'Twas seen from Dryden's groves of oak,And seen from cavern'd Hawthornden.

Seem'd all on fire that Chapel proud,Where Roslin's chiefs uncoffin'd lie;Each Baron, for a sable shroud,Sheathed in his iron panoply.

Seem'd all on fire, within, around,Deep sacristy and altar's paleShone every pillar, foliage-bound,And glimmer'd all the dead men's mail.

Blazed battlement and pinnet high,Blazed every rose-carved buttress fair;So still they blaze when Fate is nighThe lordly line of Hugh St. Clair.

But, although the last "Roslin," as he was called, died in the year 1778, and the estates passed into the possession of the Erskines, Earls of Rosslyn, the old tradition has not been extinguished. Something of the same kind is described as having happened to the old Cornish family of the Vingoes on their estate of Treville, for "through all time a peculiar token has marked the coming death of one of the family. Above the deep caverns in the Treville Cliff rises a carn. On this chains of fire were seen ascending and descending, and oftentimes were accompanied by loud and frightful noises. But it is reported that these tokens have not taken place since the last male of the family came to a violent end. According to Mr. Hunt,[42] "tradition tells us this estate was given to an old family who came with the Conqueror to this country. This ancestor is said to have been the Duke of Normandy's wine taster, and to have belonged to the ancient Counts of Treville, hence the name of the estate. For many generations the family has been declining, and the race is now nearly, if not quite, extinct.

In some cases, families have been apprised of an approaching death by some strange spectre, either male or female, a remarkable instance of which occurs in the MS. memoirs of Lady Fanshaw, and is to this effect: "Her husband, Sir Richard, and she, chanced, during their abode in Ireland, to visit a friend, who resided in his ancient baronial castle surrounded with a moat. At midnight she was awakened by a ghastly and supernatural scream, and, looking out of bed, beheld by the moonlight a female face and part of the form hovering at the window. The face was that of a young and rather handsome woman, but pale; and the hair, which was reddish, was loose and dishevelled. This apparition continued to exhibit itself for some time, and then vanished with two shrieks, similar to that which had at first excited Lady Fanshaw's attention. In the morning, with infinite terror, she communicated to her host what had happened, and found him prepared not only to credit, but to account for, what had happened.

"A near relation of mine," said he, "expired last night in the castle. Before such an event happens in this family and castle, the female spectre whom you have seen is always visible. She is believed to be the spirit of a woman of inferior rank, whom one of my ancestors degraded himself by marrying, and whom afterwards, to expiate the dishonour done his family, he caused to be drowned in the castle moat."

This, of course, was no other than the Banshee, which in times past has been the source of so much terror in Ireland. Amongst the innumerable stories told of its appearance may be mentioned one related by Mrs. Lefanu, the niece of Sheridan, in the memoirs of her grandmother, Mrs. Frances Sheridan. From this account we gather that Miss Elizabeth Sheridan was a firm believer in the Banshee, and firmly maintained that the one attached to the Sheridan family was distinctly heard lamenting beneath the windows of the family residence before the news arrived from France of Mrs. Frances Sheridan's death at Blois. She adds that a niece of Miss Sheridan's made her very angry by observing that as Mrs. Frances Sheridan was by birth a Chamberlaine, a family of English extraction, she had no right to the guardianship of an Irish fairy, and that therefore the Banshee must have made a mistake.

Likewise, many a Scotch family has its death-warning, a notable one being the Bodach Glass, which Sir Walter Scott has introduced in his "Waverley" as the messenger of bad-tidings to the MacIvors, the truth of which, it is said, has been traditionally proved by the experience of no less than three hundred years. It is thus described by Fergus to Waverley: "'You must know that when my ancestor, Ian nan Chaistel, wanted Northumberland, there was appointed with him in the expedition a sort of southland chief, or captain of a band of Lowlanders, called Halbert Hall. In their return through the Cheviots they quarrelled about the division of the great booty they had acquired, and came from words to blows. The Lowlanders were cut off to a man, and their chief fell the last, covered with wounds, by the sword of my ancestor. Since that day his spirit has crossed the Vich Ian Vohr of the day when any great disaster was impending.'" Fergus then gives to Waverley a graphic and detailed account of the appearance of the Bodach: "'Last night I felt so feverish that I left my quarters and walked out, in hopes the keen frosty air would brace my nerves. I crossed a small foot bridge, and kept walking backwards and forwards, when I observed, with surprise, by the clear moonlight, a tall figure in a grey plaid, which, move at what pace I would, kept regularly about four yards before me.'

"'You saw a Cumberland peasant in his ordinary dress, probably.'

"'No; I thought so at first, and was astonished at the man's audacity in daring to dog me. I called to him, but received no answer. I felt an anxious troubling at my heart, and to ascertain what I dreaded, I stood still, and turned myself on the same spot successively to the four points of the compass. By heaven, Edward, turn where I would, the figure was instantly before my eyes at precisely the same distance. I was then convinced it was the Bodach Glass. My hair bristled, and my knees shook. I manned myself, however, and determined to return to my quarters. My ghastly visitor glided before me until he reached the footbridge, there he stopped, and turned full round. I must either wade the river or pass him as close as I am to you. A desperate courage, founded on the belief that my death was near, made me resolve to make my way in despite of him. I made the sign of the cross, drew my sword, and uttered, 'In the name of God, evil spirit, give place!'

"'Vich Ian Vohr,' it said, in a voice that made my very blood curdle; 'beware of to-morrow.'

"'It seemed at that moment not half a yard from my sword's point; but the words were no sooner spoken than it was gone, and nothing appeared further to obstruct my passage.'"

An ancestor of the family of McClean, of Lochburg, was commonly reported, before the death of any of his race, to gallop along the sea-beach, announcing the event by dismal cries, and lamentations, and Sir Walter Scott, in his "Peveril of the Peak," tells us that the Stanley family are forewarned of the approach of death by a female spirit, "weeping and bemoaning herself before the death of any person of distinction belonging to the family."

These family death-omens are of a most varied description, having assumed particular forms in different localities. Corby Castle, Cumberland, was famed for its "Radiant Boy," a luminous apparition which occasionally made its appearance, the tradition in the family being that the person who happened to see it would rise to the summit of power, and after reaching that position would die a violent death. As an instance of this strange belief, it is related how Lord Castlereagh in early life saw this spectre; as is well-known, he afterwards became head of the government, but finally perished by his own hand. Then there was the dreaded spectre of the Goblin Friar associated with Newstead Abbey:

A monk, arrayedIn cowl and beads, and dusky garb, appeared,Now in the moonlight, and now lapsed in shade,With steps that trod as heavy, yet unheard—

This apparition was generally supposed to forebode evil to the member of the family to whom it appeared, and its movements have thus been poetically described by Lord Byron, who, it may be added, maintained that he beheld this uncanny spectre before his ill-starred union with Miss Millbanke:

By the marriage bed of their lords, 'tis said,He flits on the bridal eve;And 'tis held as faith, to their bed of deathHe comes—but not to grieve.

When an heir is born, he is heard to mourn,And when aught is to befallThat ancient line, in the pale moonshineHe walks from hall to hall.

His form you may trace, but not his face,'Tis shadowed by his cowl;But his eyes may be seen from the folds between,And they seem of a parted soul.

An ancient Roman Catholic family in Yorkshire, of the name of Middleton, is said to be apprised of the death of anyone of its members by the appearance of a Benedictine nun, and Berry Pomeroy Castle, Devonshire, was supposed to be haunted by the daughter of a former baron, who bore a child to her own father, and afterwards strangled the fruit of their incestuous intercourse. But, after death, it seems this wretched woman could not rest, and whenever death was about to visit the castle she was generally seen sadly wending her way to the scene of her earthly crimes.

According to another tradition, there is a circular tower, called "Margaret's Tower," rising above some broken steps that lead into a dismal vault, and the tale still runs that, on certain evenings in the year, the spirit of the Ladye Margaret, a young daughter of the house of Pomeroy, appears clad in white on these steps, and, beckoning to the passers-by, lures them to destruction into the dungeon ruin beneath them.

And, indeed, it would seem to have been a not infrequent occurrence for family ghosts to warn the living when death was at hand—a piece of superstition which has always held a prominent place in our household traditions, reminding us of kindred stories on the Continent, where the so-called White Lady has long been an object of dread.

There has, too, long been a strange notion that when storms, heavy rains, or other elemental strife, take place at the death of a great man, the spirit of the storm will not be appeased till the moment of burial. This belief seems to have gained great strength on the occasion of the Duke of Wellington's funeral, when, after some weeks of heavy rain, and some of the highest floods ever known, the skies began to clear, and both rain and flood abated. It was a common observation in the week before the duke's interment, "Oh, the rain won't give o'er till the Duke is buried!"

FOOTNOTES:

[39] "Family Romance"—Sir Bernard Burke—1853, ii., 200-210.

[40] In 1641 there was published a tract, with a frontispiece, entitled "A True Relation of an Apparition, in the Likeness of a Bird with a white breast, that appeared hovering over the Death-bed of some of the children of Mr. James Oxenham, &c."

[41] This tradition has been wrought into a romantic story, entitled "Chartley, or the Fatalist."

[42] "Popular Romances of West of England."

CHAPTER XI.
WEIRD POSSESSIONS.

"But not a word o' it; 'tis fairies' treasure,
Which, but revealed, brings on the blabber's ruin."

MASSINGER'S "Fatal Dowry."

From the earliest days a strange fatality has been supposed to cling to certain things—a phase of superstition which probably finds as many believers nowadays as when Homer wrote of the fatal necklace of Eriphyle that wrought mischief to all who had been in possession of it. In numerous cases, it is difficult to account for the prejudice thus displayed, although occasionally it is based on some traditionary story. But whatever the origin of the luck, or ill-luck, attaching to sundry family possessions, such heirlooms have been preserved with a kind of superstitious care, handed down from generation to generation.

One of the most remarkable curiosities connected with family superstitions is what is commonly known as "The Coalstoun Pear," the strange antecedent history of which is thus given in a work entitled, "The Picture of Scotland": "Within sight of the House of Lethington, in Haddingtonshire, stands the mansions of Coalstoun, the seat of the ancient family of Coalstoun, whose estate passed by a series of heirs of line into the possession of the Countess of Dalhousie. This place is chiefly worthy of attention here, on account of a strange heirloom, with which the welfare of the family was formerly supposed to be connected.

"One of the Barons of Coalstoun, about three hundred years ago, married Jean Hay, daughter of John, third Lord Yester, with whom he obtained a dowry, not consisting of such base materials as houses or land, but neither more nor less than a pear. 'Sure such a pear was never seen,' however, as this of Coalstoun, which a remote ancestor of the young lady, famed for his necromantic power, was supposed to have invested with some enchantment that rendered it perfectly invaluable. Lord Yester, in giving away his daughter, informed his son-in-law that, good as the lass might be, her dowry was much better, because, while she could only have value in her own generation, the pear, so long as it was continued in his family, would be attended with unfailing prosperity, and thus might cause the family to flourish to the end of time. Accordingly, the pear was preserved as a sacred palladium, both by the laird who first obtained it, and by all his descendants; till one of their ladies, taking a longing for the forbidden fruit while pregnant, inflicted upon it a deadly bite: in consequence of which, it is said, several of the best farms on the estate very speedily came to the market."

The pear, tradition goes on to tell us, became stone hard immediately after the lady had bit it, and in this condition it remains till this day, with the marks of Lady Broun's teeth indelibly imprinted on it. Whether it be really thus fortified against all further attacks of the kind or not, it is certain that it is now disposed in some secure part of the house—or as we have been informed in a chest, the key of which is kept secure by the Earl of Dalhousie—so as to be out of all danger whatsoever. The "Coalstowne pear," it is added, without regard to the superstition attached to it, must be considered a very great curiosity in its way, "having, in all probability, existed five hundred years—a greater age than, perhaps, has ever been reached by any other such production of nature."

Another strange heirloom—an antique crystal goblet—is said to have been for a long time in the possession of Colonel Wilks, the proprietor of the estate of Ballafletcher, four or five miles from Douglas, Isle of Man. It is described as larger than a common bell-shaped tumbler, "uncommonly light and chaste in appearance, and ornamented with floral scrolls, having between the designs on two sides, upright columellæ of five pillars," and according to an old tradition, it is reported to have been taken by Magnus, the Norwegian King of Man, from St. Olave's shrine. Although it is by no means clear on what ground this statement rests, there can be no doubt but that the goblet is very old. After belonging for at least a hundred years to the Fletcher family—the owners of Ballafletcher—it was sold with the effects of the last of the family, in 1778, and was bought by Robert Cæsar, Esq., who gave it to his niece for safe keeping. The tradition goes that it had been given to the first of the Fletcher family more than two centuries ago, with this special injunction, that "as long as he preserved it, peace and plenty would follow; but woe to him who broke it, as he would surely be haunted by the 'Ihiannan Shee' or 'peaceful spirit' of Ballafletcher." It was kept in a recess, whence it was never removed, except at Christmas and Eastertide, when it was "filled with wine, and quaffed off at a breath by the head of the house only, as a libation to the spirit for her protection."

Then there is the well-known English tradition relating to Eden Hall, where an old painted drinking-glass is preserved, the property of Sir George Musgrave of Edenhall, in Cumberland, in the possession of whose family it has been for many generations. The tradition is that a butler going to draw water from a well in the garden, called St. Cuthbert's well, came upon a company of fairies at their revels, and snatched it from them. They did all they could to recover their ravished property, but failing, disappeared after pronouncing the following prophecy:

If this glass do break or fallFarewell the luck of Edenhall.

So long, therefore, runs the legendary tale, as this drinking glass is preserved, the "luck of Edenhall" will continue to exist, but should ever the day occur when any mishap befalls it, this heirloom will instantly become an unlucky possession in the family. The most recent account of this cup appeared in The Scarborough Gazette in the year 1880, in which it was described as "a glass stoup, a drinking vessel, about six inches in height, having a circular base, perfectly flat, two inches in diameter, gradually expanding upwards till it ends in a mouth four inches across. The general hue is a warm green, resembling the tone known by artists as brown pink. Upon the transparent glass is traced a geometric pattern in white and blue enamel, somewhat raised, aided by gold and a little crimson." The earliest mention of this curious relic seems to have been made by Francis Douce, who was at Edenhall in the year 1785, and wrote some verses upon it, but there does not seem to be any authentic family history attaching to it.

There is a room at Muncaster Castle which has long gone by the name of Henry the Sixth's room, from the circumstance of his having been concealed in it at the time he was flying from his enemies in the year 1461, when Sir John Pennington, the then possessor of Muncaster, gave him a secret reception. When the time for the king's departure arrived, before he proceeded on his journey, he addressed Sir John Pennington with many kind and courteous acknowledgments for his loyal reception, regretting, at the same time, that he had nothing of more value to present him with, as a testimony of his goodwill, than the cup out of which he crossed himself. He then gave it into the hands of Sir John, accompanying the present with these words: "The family shall prosper so long as they preserve it unbroken." Hence it is called the "Luck of Muncaster." "The benediction attached to its security," says Roby, in his "Traditions of Lancashire," "being then uppermost in the recollection of the family, it was considered essential to the prosperity of the house at the time of the usurpation, that the Luck of Muncaster should be deposited in a safe place; it was consequently buried till the cessation of hostilities had rendered all further care and concealment unnecessary." But, unfortunately, the person commissioned to disinter the precious relic, let the box fall in which it was locked up, which so alarmed the then existing members of the family, that they could not muster courage enough to satisfy their apprehensions. The box, therefore, according to the traditionary story preserved in the family, remained unopened for more than forty years; at the expiration of which period, a Pennington, more courageous than his predecessors, unlocked the casket, and, much to the delight of all, proclaimed the Luck of Muncaster to be uninjured. It was an auspicious moment, for the doubts as to the cup's safety were now dispelled, and the promise held good:

It shall bless thy bed, it shall bless thy board,They shall prosper by this token,In Muncaster Castle good luck shall be,Till the charmed cup is broken.

Some things, again, have gained a strange notoriety through the force of circumstances. A curious story is told, for instance, of a certain iron chest in Ireland, the facts relating to which are these: In the year 1654, Mr. John Bourne, chief trustee of the estate of John Mallet, of Enmore, fell sick at his house at Durley, when his life was pronounced by a physician to be in imminent danger. Within twenty-four hours, while the doctor and Mrs. Carlisle—a relative of Mr. Bourne—were sitting by his bedside, the doctor opened the curtains at the bed-foot to give him air, when suddenly a great iron chest by the window, with three locks—in which chest were all the writings and title deeds of Mr. Mallet's estate—began to open lock by lock. The lid of the iron chest then lifted itself up, and stood wide open. It is added that Mr. Bourne, who had not spoken for twenty-four hours, raised himself up in the bed, and looking at the chest, cried out, "You say true, you say true; you are in the right; I will be with you by and bye." He then lay down apparently in an exhausted condition, and spoke no more. The chest lid fell again, and locked itself lock by lock, and within an hour afterwards Mr. Bourne expired.

There is a story current of Lord Lovat that when he was born a number of swords that hung up in the hall of the house leaped, of themselves, out of the scabbard. This circumstance often formed the topic of conversation, and, among his clan, was looked upon as an unfortunate omen. By a curious coincidence, Lord Lovat was not only the last person beheaded on Tower Hill, but was the last person beheaded in this country—April 9, 1747—an event which Walpole has thus described in one of his letters, telling us that he died extremely well, without passion, affectation, buffoonery, or timidity. He professed himself a Jansenist, made no speech, but sat down a little while in a chair on the scaffold and talked to the people about him.

And Aubrey, relating a similar anecdote of a picture, tells us how Sir Walter Long's widow did make a solemn promise to him on his death-bed that she would not marry after his decease; but this she did not keep, for "not long after, one Sir——Fox, a very beautiful young gentleman, did win her love, so that, notwithstanding her promise aforesaid, she married him. They were at South Wrathall, where the picture of Sir Walter hung over the parlour door," and, on entering this room on their return from church, the string of the picture broke, "and the picture, which was painted on wood, fell on the lady's shoulder and cracked in the fall. This made her ladyship reflect on her promise, and drew some tears from her eyes."

CHAPTER XII.
ROMANCE OF DISGUISE.

> PISANIO to IMOGEN:
> You must forget to be a woman; change
> Command into obedience: fear and niceness—
> The handmaids of all women, or, more truly,
> Woman its pretty self, into a waggish courage:
> Ready in gibes, quick answered, saucy, and
> As quarrelsome as the weasel; nay, you must
> Forget that rarest treasure of your cheek
> Exposing it—but, Oh! the harder heart!
> Alack! no remedy! to the greedy touch
> Of common-kissing Titan, and forget
> Your laboursome and dainty trims.
>
> "Cymbeline," ACT III., SC. 4.

That a woman, under any circumstances, should dismiss her proper apparel, it has been remarked, "may well appear to us as something like a phenomenon." Yet instances are far from uncommon, the motive being originated in a variety of circumstances. A young lady, it may be, falls in love, and, to gain her end, assumes male attire so that she may escape detection, as in the case of a girl, who, giving her affections to a sailor, and not being able to follow him in her natural and recognised character, put on jacket and trousers, and became, to all appearance, a brother of his mess. In other cases, a pure masculinity of character "seems to lead women to take on the guise of men. Apparently feeling themselves misplaced in, and misrepresented by, the female dress, they take up with that of men simply that they may be allowed to employ themselves in those manly avocations for which their taste and nature are fitted." In Caulfield's "Portraits of Remarkable Persons," we find a portrait of Anne Mills, styled the female sailor, who is represented as standing on what appears to be the end of a pier and holding in one hand a human head, while the other bears a sword, the instrument doubtless with which the decapitation was effected. In the year 1740, she was serving on board the Maidstone, a frigate, and in an action between that vessel and the enemy, she exhibited such desperate and daring valour as to be particularly noticed by the whole crew. But her motives for assuming the male habit do not seem to have transpired.[43]

A far more exciting career was that of Mary Anne Talbot, the youngest of sixteen illegitimate children, whom her mother bore to one of the heads of the noble house of Talbot. She was born on February 2nd, 1778, and educated under the eye of a married sister, at whose death she was committed to the care of a gentleman named Sucker, "who treated her with great severity, and who appears to have taken advantage of her friendless situation in order to transfer her, for the vilest of purposes, to the hands of a Captain Bowen, whom he directed her to look upon as her future guardian." Although barely fourteen years old, Captain Bowen made her his mistress; and, on being ordered to join his regiment at St. Domingo, he compelled the girl to go with him in the disguise of a footboy and under the name of John Taylor. But Captain Bowen had scarcely reached St. Domingo when he was remanded with his regiment to Europe to join the Duke of York's Flanders Expedition. And this time she was made to enrol herself as a drummer in the corps.

She was in several skirmishes, being wounded once by a ball which struck one of her ribs, and another time by a sabre stroke on the side. At Valenciennes, however, Captain Bowen was killed; and, finding among his effects several letters relating to herself, which proved that she had been cruelly defrauded of money left to her, she resolved to leave the regiment, and to return, if possible, to England. Accordingly she set out attired as a sailor boy, and eventually hired herself to the Commander of a French lugger, which turned out to be a privateer. But when the vessel fell in with some of Lord Howe's vessels in the Channel, she refused to fight against her countrymen, "notwithstanding all the blows and menaces the French captain could use." The privateer was taken, and our heroine was carried before Lord Howe, to whom she told candidly all that had happened to her—keeping her sex a secret.

Mary Anne Talbot, or John Taylor, was next placed on board the Brunswick, where she witnessed Lord Howe's great victory of the 1st June, and was actively engaged in it. But she was seriously wounded, "her left leg being struck a little above the knee by a musket-ball, and broken, and severely smashed lower down by a grape shot." On reaching England she was conveyed to Haslar Hospital, where she remained four months, no suspicion having ever been entertained of her being a woman. But she was no sooner out of the hospital than, retaining her disguise, she entered a small man-of-war—the Vesuvius, which was captured by two French ships, when she was sent to the prisons of Dunkirk. Here she was incarcerated for eighteen months, but, having been discovered planning an escape with a young midshipman, she was confined in a pitch-dark dungeon for eleven weeks, on a diet of bread and water. An exchange of prisoners set her at liberty, and, hearing accidentally an American merchant captain inquiring in the streets of Dunkirk for a lad to go to New York as ship's steward she offered her services, and was accepted. Accordingly, in August, 1796, she sailed with Captain Field, and, on arriving at Rhode Island, she resided with the Captain's family.

But here another kind of adventure was to befall her—for a niece of Captain Field's fell deeply in love with her, even going so far as to propose marriage. On leaving Rhode Island, the young lady had such alarming fits that, after sailing two miles, Mary Anne Talbot was called back by a boat, and compelled to promise a speedy return to the enamoured young lady. On reaching England, she was one day on shore with some of her comrades when she was seized by a press-gang, and finding there was no other way of getting off than by revealing her sex, she did so, her story creating a great sensation. From this time she never went to sea again, and soon afterwards lived in service with a bookseller, Mr. Kirby, who wrote her memoir.[44]

And the late Colonel Fred Burnaby has recorded the history of a singular case, the facts of which came under his notice when he was with Don Carlos during the Carlist rising of the year 1874: "A discovery was made a few days ago that a woman was serving in the Royalists' ranks, dressed in a soldier's uniform. She was found out in the following manner. The priest of the village to where she belonged happening to pass through a town where the regiment was quartered, and chancing to see her, was struck by the likeness she bore to one of his parishioners.

"You must be Andalicia Bravo," he remarked.

"No, I am her brother," was the reply.

The Cure's suspicions were aroused, and at his suggestion, an inquiry was made, when it was discovered that the youthful soldier had no right to the masculine vestments she wore. Don Carlos, who was told of the affair, desired that she should be sent as a nurse to the hospital of Durango, and, when he visited the establishment, presented the fair Amazon with a military cross of merit. The poor girl was delighted with the decoration, and besought the "King" to allow her to return to the regiment, as she said she was more accustomed to inflicting wounds than to healing them. In fact, she so implored to be permitted to serve once more as a soldier, that at last, Don Carlos, to extricate himself from the difficulty, said, "No, I cannot allow you to join a regiment of men; but when I form a battalion of women, I promise, upon my honour, that you shall be named the Colonel."

"It will never happen," said the girl, and she burst into tears as the King left the hospital.

At Haddon Hall may still be seen "Dorothy Vernon's Door," whence the heiress of Haddon stole out one moonlight night to join her lover. The story generally told is that, while her elder sister, the affianced bride of Sir

Thomas Stanley, second son of the Earl of Derby, was made much of in her recognised attachment, Dorothy, on the other hand, was not only kept in the background, but every obstacle was thrown in her way against a connection she had formed with John Manners, son of the Earl of Rutland. But "something of the wild bird," it is said, "was noticed in Dorothy, and she was closely watched, kept almost a prisoner, and could only beat her wings against the bars that confined her." This kind of surveillance went on for some time, but did not check the young lady's infatuation for her lover, and it was not long before the young couple contrived to see one another. Disguised as a woodman, John Manners lurked of a day in the woods round Haddon for several weeks, obtaining now and then a stolen glance, a hurried word, or a pressure of the hand from the fair Dorothy.

At length, however, an opportunity arrived which enabled Dorothy to carry out the plan which had been suggested to her by John Manners. It so happened that a grand ball was given at Haddon Hall, to celebrate the approaching marriage of the elder daughter, and, whilst a throng of guests filled the ball-room, where the stringed minstrels played old dances in the Minstrels' Gallery, and the horns blew low, everyone being too busy with his own interests and pleasures to attend to those of another, the young Miss Dorothy stole away unobserved from the ball-room, "passed out of the door, which is now one of the most interesting parts of this historic pile of buildings, and crossed the terrace to where, at the "ladies' steps," she could dimly discern figures hiding in the shadow of the trees. Another moment, and she was in her lover's arms. Horses were waiting, and Dorothy was soon riding away with her lover through the moonlight, and was married on the following morning. This story, which has been gracefully told by Eliza Meteyard under the title of "The Love Steps of Dorothy Vernon," has always been regarded as one of the most romantic and pleasant episodes in the history of Haddon Hall. Through Dorothy's marriage, the estate of Haddon passed from the family of Vernon to that of Manners, and a branch of the house of Rutland was transferred to the county of Derby."

DOROTHY VERNON AND THE WOODMAN.

But love has always been an inducement, in one form or another for disguise, and a romantic story is told of Sir John Bolle, of Thorpe Hall, in Lincolnshire, who distinguished himself at Cadiz, in the year 1596. Among the prisoners taken at this memorable seige, was "a fair captive of great beauty, high rank, and immense wealth," and who was the peculiar charge of Sir John Bolle. She soon became deeply enamoured of her gallant captor, and "in his courteous company was all her joy," her infatuation being so great that she entreated him to allow her to accompany him to England disguised as his page. But Sir John had a wife at home, and replied—to quote the version of the story given in Dr. Percy's "Relics of Ancient English Poetry":—

"Courteous lady, leave this fancy,Here comes all that breeds the strife;I in England have alreadyA sweet woman to my wife.I will not falsify my vow for gold or gain,Nor yet for all the fairest dames that live in Spain."

Thereupon the fair lady determined to retire to a convent, admiring the gallant soldier all the more for his faithful devotion to his wife.

"O happy is that womanThat enjoys so true a friend!Many happy days God send her!Of my suit I make an end,On my knees I pardon crave for my offence,Which did from love and true affection first commence.

"I will spend my days in prayer,Love and all her laws defy;In a nunnery will I shroud me,Far from any company.But ere my prayers have an end be sure of this,To pray for thee and for thy love I will not miss."

But, before forsaking the world, she transmitted to her unconscious rival in England her jewels and valuable knicknacks, including her own portrait drawn in green—a circumstance which obtained for the original the designation of the "Green Lady," and Thorpe Hall has long been said to be haunted by the lady in green, who has been in the habit of appearing beneath a particular tree close to the mansion.

A story, which has been gracefully told in one of Moore's Irish Melodies, relates to Henry Cecil, Earl of Exeter, who early in life fell in love with the rich heiress of the Vernons of Hanbury. A marriage was eventually arranged, but this union proved a complete failure, and terminated in a divorce. Thereupon young Cecil, distrustful of the conventionalities of society, and to prevent any one of the fair sex marrying him on account of his position, resolved "on laying aside the artificial attractions of his rank, and seeking some country maiden who would wed him from disinterested motives of affection."

Accordingly he took up his abode at a small inn in a retired Shropshire village, but even here his movements created suspicion, "some maintaining that he was connected with smugglers or gamesters, while all agreed that dishonesty or fraud was the cause of the mystery of the 'London gentleman's' proceedings." Annoyed at the rude molestations to which he was daily, more or less, exposed, he quitted the inn and removed to a farmhouse in the neighbourhood, where he remained for two years, in the course of which time he purchased some land, and commenced building himself a house:

But the landlord of the cottage where he lived had a beautiful daughter of about seventeen years, to whom young Cecil became so deeply attached that, in spite of her humble birth, and simple education, he resolved to make her his wife, taking an early opportunity of informing her parents of his resolve. The matter came as a surprise to the farmer and his wife, and all the more so because they had always regarded Mr. Cecil as far too grand a person to entertain such an idea.

"Marry our daughter?" exclaimed the good wife, in amazement. "What, to a fine gentleman! No, indeed!"

"Yes, marry her," added the husband, "he shall marry her, for she likes him. Has he not house and land, too, and plenty of money to keep her?"

So the rustic beauty was married, and it was not long afterwards that her husband found it necessary to repair to town on account of the Earl of Exeter's death. Setting out, as the young bride thought, on a pleasure trip, they stopped in the course of their journey at several noblemen's seats, where, to her astonishment, Cecil was welcomed in the most friendly manner. At last they reached Burleigh, in Northamptonshire—the home of the Cecils. And on driving up to the house, Cecil unconcernedly asked his wife, "whether she would like to be at home there?"

"Oh, yes," she excitedly exclaimed; "it is, indeed, a lovely spot, exceeding all I have seen, and making me almost envy its possessor."

"Then," said the young earl, "it is yours."

The whole affair seemed like a fairy tale to the bewildered girl, and who, but herself, could describe the feelings she experienced at the acclamations of joy and welcome which awaited her in her magnificent home. But it was no dream, and as soon as the young earl had arranged his affairs, he returned to Shropshire, threw off his disguise, and revealed his rank to his wife's parents, assigning to them the house he had built, with a settlement of £700 per annum.

"But," writes Sir Bernard Burke, "if report speak truly, the narrative must have a melancholy end. Her ladyship, unaccustomed to the exalted sphere in which she moved, chilled by its formalities, and depressed in her own esteem, survived only a few years her extraordinary elevation, and sank into an early grave," although Moore has given a brighter picture of this sad close to a pretty romance.

You remember Ellen, our hamlet's pride,How meekly she blessed her humble lot,When the stranger, William, had made her his bride,And love was the light of their lowly cot.Together they toiled through wind and rainTill William at length in sadness said,"We must seek our fortunes on other plains";Then sighing she left her lowly shed.

They roam'd a long and weary way,Nor much was the maiden's heart at ease,When now, at close of one stormy dayThey see a proud castle among the trees."To night," said the youth, "we'll shelter there;The wind blows cold, the hour is late";So he blew the horn with a chieftain's air,And the porter bow'd as they pass'd the gate.

"Now welcome, Lady!" exclaimed the youth;"This castle is thine, and these dark woods all."She believed him wild, but his words were truth,For Ellen is Lady of Rosna Hall!And dearly the Lord of Rosna lovesWhat William the stranger woo'd and wed;And the light of bliss in those lordly grovesIs pure as it shone in the lowly shed.

But one of the most extraordinary instances of disguise was that of the Chevalier d'Eon, who was born in the year 1728, and was an excellent scholar, soldier, and political intriguer. In the service of Louis XV., he went to Russia in female attire, obtained employment as the female reader to the Czarina Elizabeth, under which disguise he carried on political and semi-political negotiations with wonderful success. In the year 1762, he appeared in England as Secretary of the Embassy to the Duke of Nivernois, and when Louis XVI. granted him a pension and he went over to Versailles to return thanks for the favour, Marie Antoinette is said to have insisted on his assuming women's attire. Accordingly, to gratify this foolish whim, D'Eon is reported to have one day swept into the royal presence attired like a duchess, which character he supported to the great delight of the royal spectators.

In the year 1794, he returned to this country, and, being here after the Revolution was accomplished, his name was placed in the fatal list of emigrés, and he was deprived of his pension. The English Government, however, gave him an allowance of £200 a year; and in his old days he turned his fencing capabilities to account, for he occasionally appeared in matches with the Chevalier de St. George, and permanently reassumed female attire.

This eccentric character was the subject of much speculation in his lifetime, and, curious to say, in the year 1771, it was proved to the satisfaction of a jury, on a trial before Lord Chief Justice Mansfield, that the Chevalier was of the female sex. The case in question arose from a wager between Hayes, a surgeon, and Jacques, an underwriter, the latter having bound himself, on receiving a premium, to pay the former a certain sum whenever the fact was established that D'Eon was a woman. One of the witnesses was Morande, an infamous Frenchman, who gave such testimony that no human being could doubt the fact of D'Eon being of the female sex, and two French medical men gave equally conclusive evidence. The result of this absurd trial was that the jury returned a verdict for the plaintiff, with £702 damages.[45] But all doubt was cleared away when D'Eon died, in the year 1810, for, an examination of the body being made, it was publicly declared that the Chevalier was an old man. Walpole collected some facts about this remarkable man, and writes: "The Due de Choiseul believed it was a woman. After the death of Louis XV., D'Eon had leave to go to France, on which the young Comte de Guerchy went to M. de Vergennes, Secretary of State, and gave him notice that the moment D'Eon landed at Calais he, Guerchy, would cut his throat, or D'Eon should his; on which Vergennes told the Count that D'Eon was certainly a woman. Louis XV. corresponded with D'Eon, and when the Duc de Choiseul had sent a vessel, which lay six months in the Thames, to trepan and bring off D'Eon, the king wrote a letter with his own hand to give him warning of the vessel."

Like the Chevalier D'Eon, a certain individual named Russell, a native of Streatham, adopted the guise and habits of the opposite sex, and so skilfully did he keep up the deception that it was not known till after his death. It appears from Streatham Register that he was buried on April 14, 1772, the subjoined memorandum being affixed to the entry: "This person was always known under the guise or habit of a woman, and answered to the name of Elizabeth, as registered in this parish, November 21, 1669, but on death proved to be a man. It also appears from the registers of Streatham Parish, that his father, John Russell, had three daughters, and two sons— William, born in 1668, and Thomas in 1672; and there is very little doubt that the above person, who was also commonly known as Betsy the Doctress, was one of these sons."

It is said that when he assumed the garb of the softer sex he also took the name of his sister Elizabeth, who, very likely, either died in infancy, or settled at a distance; but, under this name, he applied, about two years before his death, for a certificate of his baptism. Early in life, he associated with the gypsies, and became the companion of the famous Bampfylde Moore Carew. Later on in life he resided at Chipstead, in Kent, and there catered for the miscellaneous wants of the villagers. He also visited most parts of the continent as a stroller and a vagabond, and sometimes in the company of a man who passed for his husband, he moved about from one place to another, changing his "maiden" name to that of his companion, at whose death he passed as his widow, being generally known by the familiar name of Bet Page.

According to Lysons, in the course of his wanderings he attached himself to itinerant quacks, learned their remedies, practised their calling, his knowledge, coupled with his great experience, gaining for him the reputation of being "a most infallible doctress." He also went in for astrology, and made a considerable sum of money, but was so extravagant that when he died his worldly goods were not valued at half-a-sovereign. About a year before his death he returned to his native parish, his great age bringing him into much notoriety; but his death was very sudden, and great was the surprise on all sides when it became known that he was a man. In life this strange character was a general favourite, and Mr. Thrale was wont to have him in his kitchen at Streatham Park, while Dr. Johnson, who considered him a shrewd person, held long conversations with him. To prevent the discovery of his sex he used to wear a cloth tied under his chin, and a large pair of nippers, found in his pocket after death, are supposed to have been the instruments with which he was in the habit of removing the tell-tale hairs from his face.[46]

In some instances, as in times of political intrigue and commotion, disguise has been resorted to as a means of escape and concealment of personal identity, one of the most romantic and remarkable cases on record being that of Lord Clifford, popularly known as the "shepherd lad." It appears that Lady Clifford, apprehensive lest the life of her son, seven years of age, might be sacrificed in vengeance for the blood of the youthful Earl of Rutland, whom Lord Clifford had murdered in cold blood at the termination of the battle of Sandal, placed him in the keeping of a shepherd who had married one of her inferior servants—an attendant on the boy's nurse. His name and parentage laid aside, the young boy was brought up among the moors and hills as one of the shepherd's own children. On reaching the age of fourteen, a rumour somehow spread to the Court that the son of "the black-faced Clifford," as his father had been called, was living in concealment in Yorkshire. His mother, naturally alarmed, had the boy immediately removed to the vicinity of the village of Threlkeld, amidst the Cumberland hills, where she had sometimes the opportunity of seeing him.

But, strange to say it is doubtful whether Lady Clifford made known her relationship to him, or whether, indeed, the "shepherd lord" had any distinct idea of his lofty lineage. It is generally supposed, however, that there was a complete separation between mother and child—a tradition which was accepted by Wordsworth, with whom the story of the shepherd boy was an especial favourite. In his "Song at the Feast of Brougham Castle," the poet thus prettily describes the shepherd boy's curious career:—

"Now who is he that bounds with joyOn Carroch's side, a shepherd boy?No thoughts hath he but thoughts that pass,Light as the wind along the grass.Can this be he who hither cameIn secret, like a smothered flame?O'er whom such thankful tears were shedFor shelter, and a poor man's bread!God loves the child; and God hath willedThat those dear words should be fulfilled,The lady's words, when forced away,The last she to her babe did say,'My own, my own, thy fellow guestI may not be; but rest thee, rest,For lowly shepherd's life is best.'"

Many items of traditionary lore still linger about the Cumberland hills respecting the young lord who grew up "as hardy as the heath on which he vegetated, and as ignorant as the rude herds which bounded over it." But the following description of young Clifford in his disguise, and of his employment, as given by Wordsworth, probably gives the most reliable traditionary account respecting him that prevailed in the district where he spent his lonely youth:—

"His garb is humble, ne'er was seenSuch garb with such a noble mien;Among the shepherd grooms no mateHath he, a child of strength and state!Yet lacks not friends for solemn glee,And a cheerful company,That learned of him submissive ways;And comforted his private days.To his side the fallow deerCame, and rested without fear;The eagle, lord of land and sea,Stooped down to pay him fealty;And both the undying fish that swim,Through Bowscale-Tarn did wait on him,The pair were servants to his eyeIn their immortality;They moved about in open sight,To and fro, for his delight.He knew the rocks which angels hauntOn the mountains visitant,He hath kenned them taking wing;And the caves where fairies singHe hath entered; and been toldBy voices how men lived of old."

But one of the first acts of Henry VII., on his accession to the throne was to restore young Clifford to his birthright, and to all the possessions that his distinguished sire had won. There are few authentic facts, however, recorded concerning him; for it seems that as soon as he had emerged from the hiding-place where he had been brought up in ignorance of his rank, finding himself more illiterate than was usual, even in an illiterate age, he retired to a tower, which he built in a beautiful and sequestered forest, where, under the direction of the monks of Bolton Abbey, he gave himself up to the forbidden studies of alchemy and astrology. His descendant Anne Clifford, Countess of Pembroke, describes him as "a plain man, who lived for the most part a country life, and came seldom either to Court or London, excepting when called to Parliament, on which occasion he behaved himself like a wise and good English nobleman." He was twice married, and was succeeded by his son, called Wild Henry Clifford, from the irregularities of his youth.

And we may cite the case of Matthew Hale, who, on one occasion was instrumental to justice being done through himself appearing in disguise, and supporting the wronged party. It is related that the younger of two brothers had endeavoured to deprive the elder of an estate of £500 a year by suborning witnesses to declare that he died in a foreign land. But appearing in Court in the guise of a miller, Sir Matthew Hale was chosen the twelfth juryman to sit on this cause. As soon as the clerk of the juryman had sworn in the juryman, a short dexterous fellow came into their apartment, and slipped ten gold pieces into the hands of eleven of the jury, giving the miller only five, while the judge was generally supposed to be bribed with a large sum.

At the conclusion of the case, the judge summed up the evidence in favour of the younger brother, and the jury were about to give their verdict, when the supposed miller stood up, and addressed the court. To the surprise of all present, he spoke with energetic and manly eloquence, "unravelled the sophistry to the very bottom, proved the fact of bribery, shewed the elder brother's title to the estate from the contradictory evidence of the witnesses," and in short, he gained a complete victory in favour of truth and justice.

FOOTNOTES:

[43] See "Annual Register," 1813, 1835, and 1842, for similar cases.

[44] See Notes and Queries, 6th Series, X., passim, for "Women on board ships in action"; and "Chambers's Pocket Miscellany," "Disguised Females, 1853."

[45] See "Dictionary of National Biography," xiv., 485.

[46] Arnold's "History of Streatham," 1866, 164-166. An extraordinary case of concealment of sex is recorded in the "Annual Register," under Jan. 23, 1833. An inquiry was instituted by order of the Home Secretary relative to the death of "a person who had been known for years by the name of Eliza Edwards," but who turned out to be a man.

CHAPTER XIII.
EXTRAORDINARY DISAPPEARANCES.

> "O Annie,
> It is beyond all hope, against all chance,
> That he who left you ten long years ago
> Should still be living; well, then—let me speak;
> I grieve to see you poor and wanting help:
> I cannot help you as I wish to do
> Unless—they say that women are so quick—
> Perhaps you know what I would have you know—
> wish you for my wife."
>
> Enoch Arden.

A glance at the agony columns of our daily newspapers, or the notice boards of police stations, it has been remarked, shows how many individuals disappear from home, from their business haunts, and from the circle of their acquaintances, and leave not the slightest trace of their whereabouts. In only too many instances, no satisfactory explanation has ever been forthcoming to account for a disappearance of this nature, and in the vast majority of cases no evidence has been discovered to prove the death of such persons. It is well known that "in France, before the Revolution, the vanishing of men almost before the eyes of their friends was so common that it scarcely excited any surprise at all. The only inquiry was, had he a beautiful wife or daughter, for in that case the explanation was easy; some one who had influence with the Government had designs upon the lady, and made interest to have her natural guardian put out of the way while those designs were being fulfilled." But, accountable as the disappearance of an individual was at such an unquiet time in French history, such a solution of the difficulty cannot be made to apply to our own country. Like other social problems, which no amount of intellectual ingenuity has been able to unravel, the reason why, at intervals, persons are missed and never found must always be regarded as an open question.

Thus a marriage is recorded which took place in Lincolnshire, about the year 1750. In this instance, the wedding party adjourned after the marriage ceremony to the bridegroom's residence, and dispersed, some to ramble in the garden and others to rest in the house till the dinner hour. But the bridegroom was suddenly summoned away by a domestic, who said that a stranger wished to speak to him, and henceforward he was never seen again. All kinds of inquiries were made but to no purpose, and terrible as the dismay was of the poor bride at this inexplicable disappearance of the bridegroom, no trace could be found of him. A similar tradition hangs about an old deserted Welsh Hall, standing in a wood near Festiniog. In a similar manner, the bridegroom was asked to give audience to a stranger on his wedding day, and disappeared from the face of the earth from that moment. The bride, however, seems to have survived the shock, exceeding her three score years and ten, although, it is said, during all those years, while there was light of sun or moon to lighten the earth, she sat watching—watching at one particular window which commanded a view of the approach to the house. In short, her whole faculties, her whole mental powers, became completely absorbed in that weary process of watching, and long before she died she was childish, and only conscious of one wish—to sit in that long high window, and watch the road, along which he might come. Family romance records, from time to time, many such stories, and it was not so very long ago that a bridal party were thrown into much consternation by the non-arrival of the bridegroom. Everything was in readiness, the clergy and the choir, already vested, stood in the robing room, crimson carpets were laid down from the door to the carriages; some of the guests were at the church and others at the bride's house, when an alarm was raised by the best man that the bridegroom could nowhere be found. The bride-expectant burst into a flood of tears at this cruel disappointment, especially when the ominous news reached the church that the bridegroom's wedding suit had been found in the room, laid out ready to wear, but that there was not the slightest clue as to his whereabouts. It only remained for the bridal party to return home, and for the dejected and disconsolate bride to lay aside her veil and orange-blossoms.

Sometimes, on the other hand, it is the bride who disappears at this crisis. Not many years back, an ex-lieutenant in the Royal Navy applied to a London magistrate, as he wanted to find his newly married wife. The applicant affirmed that the lady he had wedded was an actress, and that they were married at the registry office at Croydon. The magistrate asked if there had been any wedding breakfast. The applicant said "No"; they had partaken of a little luncheon and that was all. Mysterious and inexplicable as was this disappearance of a wife so shortly after marriage, it was suggested by the magistrate whether there were any rivals, but the applicant promptly replied, "No, certainly not, and that made the matter all the more incomprehensible." Of course, the magistrate could not recover the missing bride; but, remarking that the application was a very singular one, he recommended the applicant to consult the police on the matter, who replied that "he would do so, as he was really afraid that some mischief had happened to her," utterly disregarding the proposition of the magistrate as to whether the lady could not possibly have changed her mind, remarking that such a thing had occasionally happened.

In the life of Dr. Raffles, an amusing story is quoted, which is somewhat to the point: "On our way from Wem to Hawkstone, we passed a house, of which the following occurrence was told: 'A young lady, the daughter of the owner of the house, was addressed by a man who, though agreeable to her, was disliked by her father. Of course, he would not consent to their union, and she determined to disappear and elope. The night was fixed, the hour came, he placed the ladder to the window, and in a few minutes she was in his arms. They mounted a double horse, and were soon at some distance from the house. After awhile the lady broke silence by saying, 'Well, you see what a proof I have given you of my affection; I hope you will make me a good husband!'

"He was a surly fellow, and gruffly answered, 'Perhaps I may, and perhaps not.'

"She made him no reply, but, after a few minutes' silence, she suddenly exclaimed, 'O, what shall we do? I have left my money behind me in my room!'

"'Then,' said he, 'we must go and fetch it.' They were soon again at the house, the ladder was again placed, the lady remounted, while the ill-natured lover waited below. But she delayed to come, and so he gently called, 'Are you coming?' when she looked out of the window and said, 'Perhaps I may, and perhaps not,' then shut down the window, and left him to return upon the double horse alone."

But, if traditionary lore is to be believed, the sudden disappearance of the bride on her wedding day has had, in more than one instance, a very romantic and tragic origin. There is the well-known story which tells how Lord Lovel married a young lady, a baron's daughter, who, on the wedding night, proposed that the guests should play at "hide-and-seek." Accordingly, the bride hid herself in an old oak chest, but the lid falling down, shut her in, for it went with a spring lock. Lord Lovel and the rest of the company sought her that night and many days in succession, but nowhere could she be found. Her strange disappearance for many years remained an unsolved mystery, but some time afterwards the fatal chest was sold, which, on being opened, was found to contain the skeleton of the long-lost bride. This popular story was made the subject of a song, entitled "The Mistletoe Bough," by Thomas Haynes Bayley, who died in 1839; and Marwell Old Hall, near Winchester, once the residence of the Seymours, and afterwards of the Dacre family, has a similar tradition attached to it. Indeed, the very chest has been preserved in the hall of Upham Rectory, having been removed from Marwell some forty years ago. The great house at Malsanger, near Basingstoke, has a story of a like nature connected with it, reminding us of that of Tony Forster in Kenilworth, and of Rogers's Ginevra:

"There then had she found a grave!Within that chest had she concealed herself,Fluttering with joy, the happiest of the happy,When a spring lock that lay in ambush there,Fastened her down for ever."

This story is found in many places, and the chest in which the poor bride was found is shown at Bramshill, in Hampshire, the residence of Sir John Cope. But only too frequently the young lady disappears from some preconcerted arrangement; a striking instance being that of Agnes, daughter of James Ferguson, the mechanist. While walking down the Strand with her father, she slipt her hand out of his whilst he was absorbed in thought, and he never saw her from that day, nor was anything known of the girl's fate till many years after Ferguson's death. At the time, the story of her extraordinary disappearance was matter of public comment, and all kinds of extravagant theories were started to account for it. The young lady, however, was gone, and despite the most patient search, and the most persistent inquiries, no tidings could be gained as to her whereabouts. In course of years the mystery was cleared up, and revealed a pitiable case of sin and shame. It appears that a nobleman to whom she had become known at her father's lectures took her, in the first instance, to Italy, and afterwards deserted her. In her distress, being ashamed to return home, she resolved to try the stage as a means of livelihood, and applied to Garrick, who gave her a trial on the boards, but the attempt proved a failure. She then turned her hand to authorship, but with no better success. Although reduced to the most abject poverty, she would not make herself known to her relatives, and in complete despair, and overwhelmed with a sense of her disgrace, in her last extremity she threw herself on the streets, and died in miserable beggary and wretchedness in Round Court, off the Strand. It was on her death-bed that she disclosed to the surgeon who attended her the melancholy and tragic story of her wasted life. But from the localities in which she had habitually moved, she must have many a time passed her relatives in the streets, though withheld by shame from making herself known, when they imagined her to be in some distant country, or in the grave.

The strange disappearance of Lady Cathcart, on the other hand, whose fourth husband was Hugh Maguire, an officer in the Hungarian service, is an extraordinary instance of a wife being, for a long term of years, imprisoned by her own husband without any chance of escape. It seems that, soon after her last marriage, she discovered that her husband had only made her his wife with the object of possessing himself of her property, and, alarmed at the idea of losing everything, she plaited some of her jewels in her hair and others in her petticoat. But she little anticipated what was in store for her, although she had already become suspicious of her husband's intentions towards her. His plans, however, were soon executed; for one morning, under the pretence of taking her for a drive, he carried her away altogether: and when she suggested, after they had been driving some time, that they would be late for dinner, he coolly replied, "We do not dine to-day at Tewing, but at Chester, whither we are journeying."

Some alarm was naturally caused, writes Sir Bernard Burke, "by her sudden disappearance, and an attorney was sent in pursuit with a writ of habeas corpus or ne exeat regno, who found the travellers at Chester, on their way to Ireland, and demanded a sight of Lady Cathcart. Colonel Maguire at once consented, but, knowing that the attorney had never seen his wife, he persuaded a woman to personate her.

The attorney, in due time, was introduced to the supposed Lady Cathcart, and was asked if she accompanied Colonel Maguire to Ireland of her own free will. "Perfectly so," said the woman. Whereupon the attorney set out again for London, and the Colonel resumed his journey with Lady Cathcart to Ireland, where, on his arrival at his own house at Tempo, in Fermanagh, his wife was imprisoned for many years." During this period the Colonel was visited by the neighbouring gentry, "and it was his regular custom at dinner to send his compliments to Lady Cathcart, informing her that the company had the honour to drink her ladyship's health, and begging to know whether there was anything at table that she would like to eat? But the answer was always the same, "Lady Cathcart's compliments, and she has everything she wants." Fortunately for Lady Cathcart, Colonel Maguire died in the year 1764, when her ladyship was released, after having been locked up for twenty years, possessing, at the time of her deliverance, scarcely clothes to her back. She lost no time in hastening back to England, and found her house at Tewing in possession of a Mr. Joseph Steele, against whom she brought an act of ejectment, and, attending the assize in person, gained her case. Although she had been so cruelly treated by Colonel Maguire, his conduct does not seem to have injured her health, for she did not die till the year 1789, when she was in her ninety-eighth year. And, when eighty years of age, it is recorded that she took part in the gaieties of the Welwyn Assembly, and danced with the spirit of a girl. It may be added that although she survived Colonel Maguire twenty years, she was not tempted, after his treatment, to carry out the resolution which she had inscribed as a poesy on her wedding ring.

If I surviveI will have five.[47]

Another disappearance and supposed imprisonment which created considerable sensation in the last century was that of Elizabeth Canning. On New Year's Day, 1753, she visited an uncle and aunt who lived at Saltpetre Bank, near Well Close Square, who saw her part of the way home as far as Houndsditch. But as no tidings were afterwards heard of her, she was advertised for, rumours having gone abroad, that she had been heard to shriek out of a hackney coach in Bishopsgate-street. Prayers, too, were offered up for her in churches and meeting-houses, but all inquiries were in vain, and it was not until the 29th of the month that the missing girl returned in a wretched condition, ill, half-starved, and half-clad. Her story was that after leaving her uncle and aunt on the 1st of January, she had been attacked by two men in great coats, who robbed, partially stripped her, and dragged her away to a house in the Hertfordshire road, where an old woman cut off her stays, and shut her up in a room in which she had been imprisoned ever since, subsisting on bread and water, and a mince pie that her assailants had overlooked in her pocket, and ultimately, she said, she had escaped through the window, tearing her ear in doing so.

Her story created much sympathy for her, and steps were immediately taken to punish those who had abducted her in this outrageous manner. The girl, who was in a very weak condition, was taken to the house she had specified, one "Mother" Wells, who kept an establishment of doubtful reputation at Enfield Wash, and on being asked to identify the woman who had cut off her stays, and locked her up in the room referred to, pointed out one Mary Squires, an old gipsy of surpassing ugliness. Accordingly, Squires and Wells were committed for trial for assault and felony; the result of the trial being that Squires was condemned to death, and Wells to be burned in the hand, a sentence which was executed forthwith, much to the delight of the excited crowd in the Old Bailey Sessions-house.

But the Lord Mayor, Sir Crisp Gascoyne, who had presided at the trial ex-officio, was not satisfied with the verdict, and caused further and searching inquiries to be made. The verdict, on the weight of fresh evidence obtained, was upset, and Squires was granted a free pardon. On 29th April, 1754, Elizabeth Canning was summoned again to the Old Bailey, but this time to take her trial for wilful and corrupt perjury. The trial lasted eight days, and, being found guilty, she was transported in August, "at the request of her friends, to New England." According to the "Annual Register," she returned to this country at the expiration of her sentence to receive a legacy of £500, left to her three years before by an old lady of Newington Green; whereas, later accounts affirm that she never came back, but died 22nd July, 1773, at Weathersfield, in Connecticut, it being further stated that she married abroad a Quaker of the name of Treat, "and for some time followed the occupation of a schoolmistress."

The mystery of her life—her disappearance from Jan. 1st to the 29th of that month, and what transpired in that interval—is a secret that has never been to this day divulged. Indeed, as it has been observed, "notwithstanding the many strange circumstances of her story, none is so strange as that it should not be discovered in so many years where she had concealed herself during the time she had invariably declared she was at the house of Mother Wells."[48]

Another curious disappearance is recorded by Sir John Coleridge, forming a strange story of romance. It seems there lived in Cornwall, a highly respectable family, named Robinson, consisting of two sons—William and Nicholas—and two daughters. The property was settled on the two sons and their male issue, and in case of death on the two daughters. Nicholas was placed with an eminent attorney of St. Austen as his clerk, with a prospect of being one day admitted into partnership. But his legal studies were somewhat interrupted by his falling in love with a milliner's apprentice; the result being that he was sent to London to qualify himself as an attorney. But he had no sooner been admitted an attorney of the Queen's Bench and Common Pleas than he disappeared, and thenceforward he was never seen by any member of his family or former friends, all search for him proving fruitless.

In course of time the father died, and William, the elder son, succeeded to the property, dying unmarried in May, 1802. As nothing was heard of Nicholas, the two sisters became entitled to the property, of which they held possession for twenty years, no claim being made to disturb their possession of it.

But in the year 1783, a young man, whose looks and manners were above his means and situation, had made his appearance as a stranger at Liverpool, going by the name of Nathaniel Richardson—the same initials as Nicholas Robinson. He bought a cab and horse, and plied for hire in the streets of Liverpool—and being "a civil, sober, and prudent man," he soon became prosperous, and drove a coach between London and Liverpool. He married, had children, and gradually acquired considerable wealth. Having gone to Wales, however, in the year 1802, to purchase some horses, he was accidentally drowned in the Mersey. Many years after his death, it was rumoured in 1821 that this Nathaniel Richardson was no other than Nicholas Robinson, and his eldest son claimed the property, which was then inherited by the two daughters. An action was accordingly tried in Cornwall to recover the property. The strange part of the proceedings was that nearly forty years had elapsed since anyone had seen Nicholas Robinson; but, says Sir John Coleridge, "It was made out conclusively, in a most remarkable way, and by a variety of small circumstances, all pointing to one conclusion, that Nathaniel Richardson was the identical Nicholas

Robinson". The Cornish and Liverpool witnesses agreed in the description of his person, his height, the colour of his hair, his general appearance, and, more particularly, it was mentioned that he had a peculiar habit of biting his nails, and that he had a great fondness for horses.

In addition to other circumstances, there was this remarkable one—that Nathaniel's widow married again and that the furniture and effects were taken to the second husband's house. Among the articles, was an old trunk, which she had never seen opened; but, on its contents being examined one day, among other letters and papers, were found the two certificates of Nicholas Robinson's admission as Attorney to the Courts of Queen's Bench and Common Pleas—and, on the trial, the old master of Nicholas Robinson, alias Nathaniel Richardson, swore to his handwriting, and so the property was discovered.

It has been often remarked that London is about the only place in all Europe where a man, if so desirous, can disappear and live for years unknown in some secure retreat. About the year 1706, a certain Mr. Howe, after he had been married some seven or eight years, rose early one morning, and informed his wife that he was obliged to go to the Tower on special business, and at about noon the same day he sent a note to his wife informing her that business summoned him to Holland, where he would probably have to remain three weeks or a month. But from that day he was absent from his home for seventeen years, during which time his wife neither heard from him, nor of him.

His strange and unaccountable disappearance at the time naturally created comment, but no trace could be found of his whereabouts, or as to whether he had met with foul treatment. And yet the most curious part of the story remains to be told. On leaving his house in Jermyn Street, Piccadilly, Mr. Howe went no further than to a small street in Westminster, where he took a room, for which he paid five or six shillings a week, and changing his name, and disguising himself by wearing a black wig—for he was a fair man—he remained in this locality during the whole time of his absence. At the time he disappeared from his home, Mr. Howe had had two children by his wife, but these both died a few years afterwards. But, being left without the necessary means of subsistence, Mrs. Howe, after waiting two or three years in the hope of her husband's return, was forced to apply for an Act of Parliament to procure an adequate settlement of his estate, and a provision for herself out of it during his absence, as it was uncertain whether he was alive or dead. This act Mr. Howe suffered to be passed, and read the progress of it in a little coffee-house which he frequented.

After the death of her children, Mrs. Howe removed from her house in Jermyn Street to a smaller one in Brewer Street, near Golden Square. Just over against her lived one Salt, a corn chandler, with whom Mr. Howe became acquainted, usually dining with him once or twice a week. The room where they sat overlooked Mrs. Howe's dining room, and Salt, believing Howe to be a bachelor, oftentimes recommended her to him as a suitable wife. And, curious to add, during the last seven years of his mysterious absence, Mr. Howe attended every Sunday service at St. James's Church, Piccadilly, and sat in Mr. Salt's seat, where he had a good view of his wife, although he could not be easily seen by her.

At last, however, Mr. Howe made up his mind to return home, and the evening before he took this step, sent her an anonymous note requesting her to meet him the following day in Birdcage Walk, St. James's Square. At the time this billet arrived, Mrs. Howe was entertaining some friends and relatives at supper—one of her guests being a Dr. Rose, who had married her sister.

After reading the note, Mrs. Howe tossed it to Dr. Rose, laughingly remarking, "You see, brother, old as I am, I have got a gallant."

But Dr. Rose recognised the handwriting as that of Mr. Howe, which so upset Mrs. Howe that she fainted away. It was eventually arranged that Dr. Rose and his wife, with the other guests who were then at supper, should accompany Mrs. Howe the following evening to the appointed spot. They had not long to wait before Mr. Howe appeared, who, after embracing his wife, walked home with her in the most matter-of-fact manner, the two living together in the most happy and harmonious manner till death divided them.

The reason of this mysterious disappearance, Mr. Howe would never explain, but Dr. Rose often maintained that he believed his brother would never have returned to his wife had not the money which he took with him—supposed to have been from one to two thousand pounds—been all spent. "Anyhow," he used to add, "Mr. Howe must have been a good economist, and frugal in his manner of living, otherwise the money would scarce have held out."

A romance associated with Haigh Hall, in Lancashire, tells how Sir William Bradshaigh, stimulated by his love of travel and military ardour, set out for the Holy land. Ten years elapsed, and, as no tidings reached his wife of his whereabouts, it was generally supposed that he had perished in some religious crusade. Taking it for granted, therefore, that he was dead, his wife Mabel did not abandon herself to a life of solitary widowhood, but accepted an offer of marriage from a Welsh knight. But, not very long afterwards, Sir William Bradshaigh returned from his prolonged sojourn in the Holy land, and, disguised as a palmer, he visited his own castle, where he took his place amongst the recipients of Lady Mabel's bounty.

As soon, however, as Lady Mabel caught sight of the palmer, she was struck by the strong resemblance he bore to her first husband; and this impression was quickly followed by bewilderment when the mysterious stranger handed to her a ring which he affirmed had been given him by Sir William, in his dying moments, to bear to his wife at Haigh Hall.

In a moment Lady Mabel's thoughts travelled back into the distant past, and she burst into tears as the ring brought back the dear memories of bygone days. It was in vain she tried to stifle her feelings, and, as her second husband—the Welsh Knight—looked on and saw how distressed she was, "he grew," says the old record, "exceeding wroth," and, in a fit of jealous passion, struck Lady Mabel.

This ungallant act was the climax of the painful scene, for there and then Sir William threw aside his disguise, and hastened to revenge the unchivalrous conduct of the Welsh knight. Completely confounded at this unexpected turn of events, and fearing violence from Sir William, the Welsh knight rode off at full speed, without waiting for any explanation of the matter. But he was overtaken very speedily and slain by his opponent, an offence for which Sir William was outlawed for a year and a day; while Mabel, his wife, "was enjoined by her confessor to do penance by going once every week, barefoot and bare legged, to a cross near Wigan, popularly known as Mab's Cross.[49]

In Wigan Parish Church, two figures of whitewashed stone preserve the memory of Sir William Bradshaigh and his Lady Mabel, he in an antique coat of mail, cross-legged, with his sword, partly drawn from the scabbard, by his left side, and she in a long robe, veiled, her hands elevated and conjoined in the attitude of fervent prayer. Sir Walter Scott informs us that from this romance he adopted his idea of "The Betrothed," "from the edition preserved in the mansion of Haigh Hall, of old the mansion house of the family of Bradshaigh, now possessed by their descendants on the female side, the Earls of Balcarres."[50]

LADY MABEL AND THE PALMER.

Scottish tradition ascribes to the Clan of Tweedie a descent of a similar romantic nature. A baron, somewhat elderly, had wedded a buxom young wife, but some months after their union he left her to ply the distaff among the mountains of the county of Peebles, near the sources of the Tweed. After being absent seven or eight years—no uncommon space for a pilgrimage to Palestine—he returned, and found, to quote the account given by Sir Walter Scott, "his family had not been lonely in his absence, the lady having been cheered by the arrival of a stranger who hung on her skirts and called her mammy, and was just such as the baron would have longed to call his son, but that he could by no means make his age correspond with his own departure for Palestine. He applied, therefore, to his wife for the solution of the dilemma, who, after many floods of tears, informed her husband that, walking one day along the banks of the river, a human form arose from a deep eddy, termed Tweed-pool, who deigned to inform her that he was the tutelar genius of the stream, and he became the father of the sturdy fellow whose appearance had so much surprised her husband." After listening to this strange adventure, "the husband believed, or seemed to believe, the tale, and remained contented with the child with whom his wife and the Tweed had generously presented him. The only circumstance which preserved the memory of the incident was that the youth retained the name of Tweed or Tweedie." Having bred up the young Tweed as his heir while he lived, the baron left him in that capacity when he died, "and the son of the river-god founded the family of Drummelzier and others, from whom have flowed, in the phrase of the Ettrick shepherd, 'many a brave fellow, and many a bauld feat.'"

It may be added that, in some instances, the science of the medical jurist has aided in elucidating the history of disappearances, through identifying the discovered remains with the presumed missing subjects. Some years ago, the examination of a skeleton found deeply imbedded in the sand of the sea-coast at a certain Scotch watering-place showed that the person when living must have walked with a very peculiar and characteristic gait, in consequence of some deposits of a rheumatic kind which affected the lower part of the spine. The mention of this circumstance caused a search to be made through some old records of the town, and resulted in the discovery of a mysterious disappearance, which, at the time, had been duly noted—the subject being a person whose mode of walking had made him an object of attention, and whose fate, but for the observant eye of the anatomist, must have remained wholly unknown. Similarly, it has been pointed out how skeletons found in mines, in disused wells, in quarries, in the walls of ruins, and various other localities "imply so many social mysteries which probably occasioned in their day a wide-spread excitement, or at least agitated profoundly some small circle of relatives or friends." According to the "Annual Register" (1845, p. 195), while some men were being employed in taking the soil from the bottom of the river in front of some mills a human skeleton was accidentally found. At a coroner's inquest, it transpired that about nine years before a Jew whose name was said to be Abrams, visited Taverham in the course of his business, sold some small articles for which he gave credit to the purchasers, and left the neighbourhood on his way to Drayton, the next village, with a sum of £90 in his possession. But at Drayton he disappeared, and never returned to Taverham to claim the amount due to him.

Search was made for the missing man, but to no purpose, and after the excitement in the neighbourhood had abated, the matter was soon forgotten. But some time afterwards a man named Page was apprehended for sheep stealing, tried, and sentenced to be transported for life. During his imprisonment, he told divers stories of robberies and crimes, most of which turned out to be false. But, amongst other things, he wrote a letter promising that if he were released from gaol and brought to Cossey, "he would show them that, from under the willow tree, which would make every hair in their heads rise up." The man was not released, but the river was drawn, and some sheep's skins and sheep's heads were found, which were considered to be the objects alluded to by Page. The search, however, was still pursued, and from under the willow tree the skeleton was fished up, evidently having been fastened down. It was generally supposed that these were the bones of the long lost Jew, who, no doubt, had been murdered for the money on his person—a crime of which Page was aware, if he were not an accomplice.

FOOTNOTES:

[47] See "Romantic Records of the Arisracy," 1850, I., 83-87.

[48] See "Dict. of Nat. Biog.," VIII., 418-420; Caulfield's "Remarkable Persons," and Gent. Mag., 1753 and 1754.

[49] Sir B. Burke's "Vicissitudes of Families," first series, 270-273. Harland's "Lancashire Legends," 45-47. Roby's "Traditions of Lancashire."

[50] The tale of the noble Moringer is, in some respects, almost identical with this tradition. It exists in a collection of German popular songs, and is supposed to be extracted from a manuscript "Chronicle of Nicholas Thomann, Chaplain to St. Leonard in Weissenhorn," and dated 1533.

CHAPTER XIV.
HONOURED HEARTS.

> "I will ye charge, after that I depart
> To holy grave, and thair bury my heart,
> Let it remaine ever bothe tyme and hour,
> To ye last day I see my Saviour."
>
> —Old ballad quoted in Sir Walter Scott's notes to "Marmion."

A curious and remarkable custom which prevailed more or less down to the present century was that of heart burial. In connection with this strange practice numerous romantic stories are told, the supreme regard for the heart as the source of the affections, having caused it to be bequeathed by a relative or friend, in times past, as the most tender and valuable legacy. In many cases, too, the heart, being more easy to transport, was removed from some distant land to the home of the deceased, and hence it found a resting place, apart from the body, in a locality endeared by past associations.

Westminster Abbey, it may be remembered, contains the hearts of many illustrious personages. The heart of Queen Elizabeth was buried there, and it is related how a prying Westminster boy one day, discovering the depositories of the hearts of Elizabeth and her sister, Queen Mary, subsequently boasted how he had grasped in his hand those once haughty hearts. Prince Henry of Wales, son of James I., who died at the early age of eighteen, was interred in Westminster Abbey, his heart being enclosed in lead and placed upon his breast, and among further royal personages whose hearts were buried in a similar manner may be mentioned Charles II., William and Mary, George, Prince of Denmark, and Queen Anne.

The heart of Edward, Lord Bruce, was enclosed in a silver case, and deposited in the abbey church of Culross, near the family seat. In the year 1808, this sad relic was discovered by Sir Robert Preston, the lid of the silver case bearing on the exterior the name of the unfortunate duellist; and, after drawings had been taken of it, the whole was carefully replaced in the vault; and in St. Nicholas's Chapel, Westminster, was enshrined the heart of Esme Stuart, Duke of Richmond, where a monument to his memory is still to be seen with this fact inscribed upon it.

Many interesting instances of heart burial are to be found in our parish churches. In the church of Horndon-on-the-Hill, Essex, which was once the seat of Sir Thomas Boleyn, a nameless black marble monument is pointed out as that of Anne Boleyn. According to a popular tradition long current in the neighbourhood, this is said to have contained the head, or heart. "It is within a narrow seat," writes Miss Strickland, "and may have contained her head, or her heart, for it is too short to contain a body. The oldest people in the neighbourhood all declare that they have heard the tradition in their youth from a previous generation of aged persons, who all affirm it to be Anne Boleyn's monument." But, it would seem, there has always been a mysterious uncertainty about Anne Boleyn's burial place, and a correspondent of the Gentleman's Magazine (October, 1815), speaks of "the headless remains of the departed queen, as deposited in the arrow chest and buried in the Tower Chapel before the high altar. Where that stood, the most sagacious antiquary, after a lapse of more than 300 years, cannot now determine; nor is the circumstance, though related by eminent writers, clearly ascertained. In a cellar, the body of a person of short stature, without a head, not many years since, was found, and supposed to be the reliques of poor Anne, but soon after it was reinterred in the same place and covered with earth."[51]

By her testament, Eleanor, Duchess of Buckingham, wife of Edward, Duke of Buckingham, who was beheaded on May 17th, 1521, appointed her heart to be buried in the church of the Grey Friars, within the City of London; and in the Sackville Vault, in Withyam Church, Sussex, is a curiously shaped leaden box in the form of a heart, on a brass plate attached to which is this inscription: "The heart of Isabella, Countess of Northampton, died on October 14th, 1661." A leaden drum deposited in a vault in the church of Brington is generally supposed to contain the head of Henry Spencer, Earl of Sunderland, who received his death wound at the battle of Newbury; and at Wells Cathedral, in a box of copper, a heart was accidentally discovered, supposed to be that of one of the bishops; and in the family vault of the Hungerfords, at Farley Castle, a heart was one day found in a glazed earthenware pot, covered with white leather. The widow of John Baliol, father of Bruce's rival, showed her affection for her dead lord in a strange way, for she embalmed his heart, placed it in an ivory casket, and during her twenty years of widowhood she never sat down to meals without this silent reminder of happier days. On her death, she left instructions for her husband's heart to be laid on her bosom, and from that day "New Abbey" was known as Sweet Heart Abbey, and "never," it is said, "did abbey walls shelter a sweeter, truer heart than that of the lady of Barnard Castle."

Among the many instances of heart-bequests may be noticed that of Edward I., who on his death-bed expressed a wish to his son that his heart might be sent to Palestine, inasmuch as after his accession he had promised to return to Jerusalem, and aid the crusade which was then in a depressed condition. But, unfortunately, owing to his wars with Scotland, he failed to fulfil his engagement, and at his death he provided two thousand pounds of silver for an expedition to convey his heart thither, "trusting that God would accept this fulfilment of his vow, and grant his blessing on the undertaking"; at the same time imprecating "eternal damnation on any who should expend the money for any other purpose." But his injunction was not performed.

Robert Bruce, king of Scotland, the avowed foe of Edward I., also gave directions to his trusted friend, Sir James Douglas, that his heart should be buried in the Holy Land, because he had left unfulfilled a vow to assist in the Crusade, but his wish was frustrated owing to the following tragic occurrence. After the king's death, his heart was taken from his body, and, enclosed in a silver case, was worn by Sir James Douglas suspended to his neck, who set out for the Holy Land. On reaching Spain, he found the King of Castile engaged in war with the Moors, and thinking any contest with Saracens consistent with his vows, he joined the Spaniards against the Moors. But being overpowered by the enemy's horsemen, in desperation he took the heart from his neck, and threw it before him, shouting aloud, "Pass on as thou wert wont, I will follow or die." He was almost immediately struck down, and under his body was found the heart of Bruce, which was intrusted to the charge of Sir Simon Locard of Lee, who conveyed it back to Scotland, and interred it beneath the high altar in Melrose Abbey, in connection with which Mrs. Hemans wrote some spirited lines:—

Heart! thou didst press forward stillWhen the trumpet's note rang shrill,Where the knightly swords were crossingAnd the plumes like seafoam tossing.Leader of the charging spear,Fiery heart—and liest thou here?May this narrow spot inurnAught that so could heat and burn?

The heart of Richard, the Lion-hearted, has had a somewhat eventful history. It seems that this monarch bequeathed his heart to Rouen, as a lasting recognition of the constancy of his Norman subjects. The honour was gratefully acknowledged, and in course of time a beautiful shrine was erected to his memory in the cathedral. But this costly structure did not escape being destroyed in the year 1738 with other Plantagenet memorials. A hundred years afterwards the mutilated effigy of Richard was discovered under the cathedral pavement, and near it the leaden casket that had inclosed his heart, which was replaced. Before long it was taken up again, and removed to the Museum of Antiquities, where it remained until the year 1869, when it found a more fitting resting-place in the choir of the cathedral.

James II. bequeathed his heart to be buried in the Church of the Convent Dames de St. Marie, at Chaillot, whence it was afterwards removed to the chapel of the English Benedictines in the Faubourg St. Jacques. And the heart of Mary Beatrice, his wife, was also bequeathed to the Monastery of Chaillot, in perpetuity, "to be placed in the tribune beside those of her late husband, King James, and the Princess, their daughter." Dr. Richard Rawlinson, the well known antiquary bequeathed his heart to St. John's College, Oxford; and Edward, Lord Windsor, of Bradenham, Bucks, who died at Spa in the year 1754, directed that his body should be buried in the "Cathedral church of the noble city of Liege, with a convenient tomb to his memory, but his heart to be enclosed in lead and sent to England, there to be buried in the chapel of Bradenham, under his father's tomb, in token of a true Englishman."

Paul Whitehead, who died in the year 1774, left his heart to his friend Lord le Despencer, to be deposited in his mausoleum at West Wycombe. Lord le Despencer accepted the bequest, and on the 16th May, 1775, the heart, after being wrapped in lead and placed in a marble urn, was carried with much ceremony to its resting place. Preceding the bier bearing the urn, "a grenadier marched in full uniform, nine grenadiers two deep, the odd one last; two German flute players, two surpliced choristers with notes pinned to their backs, two more flute players, eleven singing men in surplices, two French horn players, two bassoon players, six fifers, and four drummers with muffled drums. Lord le Despencer, as chief mourner, followed the bier, in his uniform as Colonel of the Bucks Militia, and was succeeded by nine officers of the same corps, two fifers, two drummers, and twenty soldiers with their firelocks reversed. The Dead March in "Saul" was played, the church bell tolled, and cannons were discharged every three and a half minutes." On arriving at the mausoleum, another hour was spent by the procession in going round and round it, singing funeral dirges, after which the urn containing the heart was carried inside, and placed upon a pedestal bearing the name of Paul Whitehead, and these lines:

Unhallowed hands, this urn forbear;No gems, no Orient spoil,Lie here concealed; but what's more rare,A heart that knew no guile.

But in the year 1829 some unhallowed hand stole the urn, and the whereabouts of Whitehead's heart remains a mystery to the present day. In recent times an interesting case of heart burial was that of Lord Byron, whose heart was enclosed in a silver urn and placed at Newstead Abbey in the family vault; and another was that of the poet, Shelley, whose body, according to Italian custom after drowning, was burnt to ashes. But the heart would not consume, and so was deposited in the English burying ground at Rome.

It is worthy, too, of note that heart burial prevailed to a very large extent on the Continent. To mention a few cases, the heart of Philip, King of Navarre, was buried in the Jacobin's Church, Paris, and that of Philip, King of France, at the convent of the Carthusians at Bourgfontaines, in Valois. The heart of Henri II., King of France, was enshrined in an urn of gilt bronze in the Celestins, Paris; that of Henri III., according to Camden, was enclosed in a small tomb, and Henri IV.'s heart was buried in the College of the Jesuits at La Fleche. Heart burial, again, was practised at the deaths of Louis IX., XII., XIII., and XIV., and in the last instance was the occasion of an imposing ceremony. "The heart of this great monarch," writes Miss Hartshorne, "was carried to the Convent of the Jesuits. A procession was arranged by the Cardinal de Rohan, and, surrounded by flaming torches and escorted by a company of the Royal Guards, the heart arrived at the convent, where it was received by the rector, who pronounced over it an eloquent and striking discourse."

The heart of Marie de Medicis, who built the magnificent palace of the Luxembourg, was interred at the Church of the Jesuits, in Paris; and that of Maria Theresa, wife of Louis XIV., was deposited in a silver case in the monastery of Val de Grace. The body of Gustavus Adolphus, the illustrious monarch who fell in the field of Lutzen, was embalmed, and his heart received sepulchre at Skholm; and, as is well known, the heart of Cardinal Mazarin was, by his own desire, sent to the Church of the Theatins. And Anne of Austria, the mother of Louis XIV., directed in her will that her body should be buried at St. Denis near to her husband, "of glorious memory," but her heart she bequeathed to Val de Grace; and she also decreed that it should be drawn out through her side without making any further opening than was absolutely necessary. Instances such as these show the prevalence of the custom of heart burial in bygone times, a further proof of which may be gathered from the innumerable effigies or brasses in which a heart holds a prominent place.

FOOTNOTES:

[51] See Timbs' "Abbeys, Castles, and Ancient Halls of England," i., p. 300; and "Enshrined Hearts of Warriors and Illustrious People," by Emily Sophia Hartshorne, 1861.

CHAPTER XV.
ROMANCE OF WEALTH.

> The unsunn'd heaps
> Of miser's treasure.
>
> MILTON.

Stories of lost or unclaimed property have always possessed a fascinating charm, but, unfortunately, the links for proving the rightful ownership break off generally at the point where its history seems on the verge of being unravelled. At the same time, however romantic and improbable some of the announcements relating to such treasure-hoards may seem, there is no doubt that many a poor family, at the present day, would be possessed of great wealth if it could only gain a clue to the whereabouts of money rightfully its own.

The legal identification, too, of such property when discovered has frequently precluded its successfully being claimed by those really entitled to enjoy it, and few persons are aware of the enormous amount of unclaimed money—amounting to some millions—which lies dormant, although continually made public in the "agony columns" of the Times and other daily newspapers. It should be also remembered that wealth of this kind is carefully preserved in all kinds of places; bankers' cellars, for instance, containing some of the most curious unclaimed deposits, many of them being of rare intrinsic value, whilst others are of great romantic interest.

Thus, not many years ago, there was accidentally discovered in the vaults of the Bank of England a large chest of some considerable age, which, on being removed from its resting place, almost fell to pieces. On the contents of this old chest being examined, some massive plate of the time of Charles II. was brought to light, of very beautiful and chaste workmanship. Nor was this all, for much to the surprise of the explorers, a bundle of love letters, written during the period of the Restoration, was found carefully packed away with the plate. On search being made by the directors of the bank in their books, the surviving heir of the original depositor was ascertained, to whom the plate and packet of love letters were handed over.

Many similar cases might be quoted, for in most of our bank cellars are hoarded away family treasures, which for some inexplicable reason have never been claimed. Some, again, of our old jewellers' shops have had strange deposits in their cellars, the history and whereabouts of their owners having baffled the most searching and minute inquiries. As an illustration, may be given an instance which occurred some years back in connection with a jeweller's shop near Soho. It seems that an old lady lodged for a few weeks over the said shop, and, on leaving for the Continent, left behind her, for safety's sake, several boxes of plate to be taken care of until further notice. But years passed by and no tidings of the lady reached the jeweller, although from time to time the most careful inquiries were instituted. At last, however, it transpired that she had died somewhat suddenly, but, as no record was found amongst her papers relating to the boxes of plate, a lengthened litigation arose as to the rightful claimant of the property.

Occasionally, through domestic differences, homes are broken up and the members dispersed, some perhaps going abroad. In many cases, such persons it may be are not only lost sight of for years, but are never heard of again, and hence, when they become entitled to money, large sums are frequently spent in advertising for their whereabouts, and oftentimes with no satisfactory results. Indeed, advertisements for missing relatives are, it is said, yearly on the increase, and considerable sums of money cannot be touched owing to the uncertainty as to whether persons of this description are alive or dead. An interesting instance occurred in the year 1882, when Sir James Hannen had the following case brought before him: "Counsel applied on behalf of Augustus Alexander de Niceville for letters of administration to the property of his father, supposed to be dead, as he had not been heard of since the year 1831, and who, if alive, would be 105 years old. In early life he held a commission in the French army, but in the year 1826 he came to this country and settled in Devonshire. On the breaking out of the French Revolution he returned with his wife to France, but his wife came back to England, and corresponded with her husband till the year 1831, when she ceased to hear from him. In spite of every means employed for tracing his whereabouts, nothing was ever heard of him, his wife dying in the year 1875. Affidavits in support of these facts having been read, the application was granted."

Then there are the well-known unclaimed funds in Chancery, concerning which so much interest attaches. It may not be generally known what a mine of wealth these dormant funds constitute, amounting to many millions; indeed, the Royal Courts of Justice have been mainly built with the surplus interest of this money, and occasionally large sums from this fund have been borrowed to enable the Chancellor of the Exchequer to carry through his financial operations. By an Act passed in the year 1865, facilities are afforded to apply £1,000,000 from funds standing in the books of the Bank of England to an account thus designated: "Account of securities purchased with surplus interest arising from securities carried to the account of moneys placed out for the benefit and better security of the suitors of the Court of Chancery." Not so very long ago the subject was discussed in Parliament, when it was urged that, as the Government were trustees of these funds, something should be done, as far as possible, by publicity, to adopt measures whereby the true owners might become claimants if they had but the knowledge of their rights.

Another reason for money remaining unclaimed for a number of years, is through missing wills. Hence many a family forfeits its claim to certain property on account of the testator's last wishes not being forthcoming. Thackeray makes one of his plots hang in a most ingenious way upon a missing will, which is discovered eventually in the sword-box of a family coach, and various curious instances are on record of wills having been discovered years after the testator's death in the most out-of-the-way and unlikely hiding places. In some cases, also, through a particular clause in a will being peculiarly or doubtfully worded, heirs have been deprived of what was really due to them, a goodly part of the property having been squandered and wasted in prolonged legal expenses.

Then, again, it is universally acknowledged that there is an immense quantity of money, and other valuables, concealed in the earth. In olden days, the householder was the guardian of his own money, and so had to conceal it as his ingenuity could devise. Accordingly large sums of money were frequently buried underground, and in excavating old houses, treasures of various kinds are oftentimes found underneath the floors. The custom of making the earth a stronghold, and confiding to its safe-keeping deposits of money, prevailed until a comparatively recent period, and was only natural, when it is remembered how, in consequence of civil commotions, many a home was likely to be robbed of its most valuable belongings. Hence every precaution was taken, a circumstance which accounts for the cunning secretal of rich and costly relics in old buildings. According to an entry given by Pepys in his "Diary," a large amount was supposed to be buried in his day, and he gives an amusing account of the hiding of his own money by his wife and father when the Dutch fleet was supposed to be in the Medway. Times of trouble, therefore, will account for many of the treasures which were so carefully secreted in olden times. Many years ago, as the foundations of some old houses in Exeter were being removed, a large collection of silver coins was discovered—the money found dating from the time of Henry VIII. to Charles I., or the Commonwealth—and it has been suggested that the disturbed state of affairs in the middle of the 17th century led to this mode of securing treasure.

This will account in some measure for the traditions of the existence of large sums of hidden money associated with some of our old family mansions. An amusing story is related by Thomas of Walsingham, which dates as far back as the 14th century. A certain Saracen physician came to Earl Warren to ask permission to kill a dragon which had its den at Bromfield, near Ludlow, and committed great ravages in the earl's lands. The dragon was overcome; but it transpired that a large treasure lay hid in its den. Thereupon some men of Herefordshire went by night to dig for the gold, and had just succeeded in reaching it when the retainers of the Earl of Warren, having learnt what was going on, captured them and took possession of the hoard for the earl. A legend of this kind was long connected with Hulme Hall, formerly a seat of a branch of the Prestwich family. It seems that during the civil wars its then owner, Sir Thomas Prestwich, was very much impoverished by fines and sequestrations, so that he was forced to sell the mansion and estate to Sir Oswald Mosley. On more than one occasion his mother had induced him to advance large sums of money to Charles I. and his adherents, under the assurance that she had hidden treasures which would amply repay him. This hoard was generally supposed to have been hidden, either in the hall itself, or in the grounds adjoining, and it was said to be protected by spells and incantations, known only to the lady dowager herself. Time passed on, and the old lady became every day more infirm, and at last she was struck down with apoplexy before she could either practise the requisite incantations, or inform her son where the treasure was secreted. After her burial, diligent search was made, but to no effect; and Sir Thomas Prestwich went down to the grave in comparative poverty. Since that period fortune-tellers and astrologers have tried their powers to discover the whereabouts of this hidden hoard, and, although they have been unsuccessful, it is still believed that one day their labours will be rewarded, and that the demons who guard the money will be forced to give up their charge. Some years ago the hall and estate were sold to the Duke of Bridgewater, and, the site having been required for other purposes, the hall was pulled down, but no money was discovered.

In Ireland, there are few old ruins in and about which excavations have not been made in the expectation of discovering hidden wealth, and in some instances the consequence of this belief has been the destruction of the building, which has been actually undermined. About three miles south of Cork, near the village of Douglas, is a hill called Castle Treasure, where a "cross of gold" was supposed to be concealed; and the discovery, some years ago, of a rudely-formed clay urn and two or three brazen implements attracted for some time crowds to the spot.

But such stories are not confined to any special locality, and there is, in most parts of England, a popular belief that vast treasures are hidden beneath the old ruins of many houses, and that supernatural obstacles always prevent their being discovered. Indeed, Scotland has numerous legends of this kind, some of which, as Mr. Chambers has pointed out, have been incorporated into its popular rhymes. Thus, on a certain farm in the parish of Lesmahagow, from time immemorial there existed a tradition that underneath a very large stone was secreted a vast treasure in the shape of a kettleful, a bootful, and a bull-hide full "of gold, all of which have been designated 'Katie Neevie's hoord,'" having given rise to the following adage:

Between Dillerhill and CrossfordThere lies Katie Neevie's hoord.

And at Fardell, anciently the seat of Sir Walter Raleigh's family, in the courtyard formerly stood an inscribed bilingual stone of the Roman British period; the stone is now in the British Museum. The tradition current in the neighbourhood makes the inscription refer to a treasure buried by Sir Walter Raleigh, and hence the local rhyme:

Between this stone and Fardell HallLies as much money as the devil can haul.

A curious incident happened in Ireland about the commencement of the last century. The Bishop of Derry being at dinner, there came in an old Irish harper, and sang an ancient song to his harp. The Bishop, not being acquainted with Irish, was at a loss to understand the meaning of the song, but on inquiry he ascertained the substance of it to be this—that in a certain spot a man of gigantic stature lay buried, and that over his breast and back were plates of pure gold, and on his fingers rings of gold so large that an ordinary man might creep through them. The spot was so exactly described that two persons actually went in quest of the garden treasure. After they had dug for some time, they discovered two thin pieces of gold, circular, and more than two inches in diameter. But when they renewed their excavations on the following morning they found nothing more. The song of the harper has been identified as "Moiva Borb," and the lines which suggested the remarkable discovery have been translated thus:

In earth, beside the loud cascade,The son of Sora's king we laid;And on each finger placed a ringOf gold, by mandate of our king.

The loud cascade was the well-known waterfall at Ballyshannon, known as "The Salmon Leap" now.

THERE CAME IN AN OLD IRISH HARPER
AND SANG AN ANCIENT SONG TO HIS HARP.

It was also a common occurrence for a miser to hide away his hoards underground, and before he had an opportunity of making known their whereabouts he died, without his heirs being put in the necessary possession of the information regarding that part of the earth wherein he had kept secreted his wealth. At different times, in old houses have been discovered misers' hoards, and which, but for some accident, would have remained buried in their forgotten resting-place. This will frequently account for money being found in the most eccentric nooks, an illustration of which happened a few years ago in Paris, when a miser died, leaving behind him, as was supposed, money to the value of sixty pounds. After some months had passed by, the claimant to the property made his appearance, and, on the miser's apartments being thoroughly searched, no small astonishment was caused by the discovery of the large sum of thirty-two thousand pounds. It may be noted that in former years our forefathers were extremely fond of hiding away their money for safety, making use of the chimney, or the wainscot or skirting-board. There it frequently remained; and such depositories of the family wealth were occasionally, from death and other causes, completely forgotten. In one of Hogarth's well-known pictures, the young spendthrift, who has just come into his inheritance, is being measured by a fashionable tailor, when, from behind the panels which the builders are ripping down, is seen falling a perfect shower of golden money.

There can be no doubt that there is many an old house in this country which, if thoroughly ransacked, would be found to contain treasures of the most valuable and costly kind. Some years ago, for example, a collection of pictures was discovered at Merton College, Oxford, hidden away between the ceiling and the roof; and missing deeds have from time to time been discovered located in all sorts of mysterious nooks. In a set of rooms in Magdalen College, too, which had been originally occupied by one of the Fellows, and had subsequently been abandoned and devoted to lumber, was unearthed a strong wooden box, containing, together with some valuable articles of silver plate, a beautiful loving-cup, with a cover of pure gold. When, also, the Vicarage house of Ormesby, in Yorkshire, required reparation, some stonework had to be removed in order to carry out the necessary alterations, in the course of which a small box was found, measuring about a foot square, which had been embedded in the wall. The box, when opened, was full of angels, angelets, and nobles. Some of the money was of the reign of Edward IV., some of Henry VI., and some, too, of the reigns of Henry VII. and Henry VIII. It has been suggested that when Henry VIII. dissolved the lesser monasteries, the monks of Guisboro' Priory, which was only about six miles off, fearing the worst, fled with their treasures, and, with the craft and cunning peculiar to their order, buried a portion of them in the walls of the parsonage house of Ormesby.[52]

To quote another case, Dunsford, in his "Memories of Tiverton" (1790), p. 285, speaking of the village of Chettiscombe, says that in the middle of the 16th century, in the north part of this village was "a chapel entire, dedicated to St. Mary. The walls and roof are still whole, and served some years past for a dwelling-house, but is now uninhabited." It appears that not only was there some superstition attaching to this building, which accounted for its untenanted condition, but certain money was supposed to be hidden away, to discover which every attempt had hitherto been in vain. "It was therefore proposed," says the author, "that some person should lodge in the chapel for a night to obtain preternatural information respecting it. Two persons at length complied with the request to do so, and, aided by strong beer, approached about nine o'clock the hallowed walls. They trembled exceedingly at the sudden appearance of a white owl that flew from a broken window with the message that considerable wealth lay in certain fields, that if they would diligently dig there, they would undoubtedly find it." They quickly attended to this piece of information, and employed a body of workmen who, before long, succeeded in bringing to light the missing money.

A similar tradition was associated with Bransil Castle, a stronghold of great antiquity, situated in a romantic position about two miles from the Herefordshire Beacon. The story goes that the ghost of Lord Beauchamp, who died in Italy, could never rest until his bones were delivered to the right heir of Bransil Castle. Accordingly, they were sent from Italy enclosed in a small box, and were for a considerable time in the possession of Mr. Sheldon, of Abberton. The tradition further states that the old Castle of Bransil was moated round, and in that moat a black crow, presumed to be an infernal spirit, sat to guard a chest of money, till discovered by the rightful owner. The chest could never be moved without the mover being in possession of the bones of Lord Beauchamp.

Such stories of hidden wealth being watched over by phantom beings are not uncommon, and remind us of those anecdotes of treasures concealed at the bottom of wells, guarded over by the "white ladies." In Shropshire, there is an old buried well of this kind, at the bottom of which a large hoard has long been supposed to lie hidden, or as a local rhyme expresses it:

Near the brook of BellThere is a wellWhich is richer than any man can tell.

In the South of Scotland it is the popular belief that vast treasures have for many a year past been concealed beneath the ruins of Hermitage Castle; but, as they are supposed to be in the keeping of the Evil One, they are considered beyond redemption. At different times various efforts have been made to dig for them, yet "somehow the elements always on such occasions contrived to produce an immense storm of thunder and lightning, and deterred the adventurers from proceeding, otherwise, of course the money would long ago have been found." And to give another of these strange family legends, may be quoted one told of Stokesay Castle, Shropshire. It seems that many years ago all the country in the neighbourhood of Stokesay belonged to two giants, who lived the one upon View Edge, and the other at Norton Camp. The story commonly current is that "they kept all their money locked up in a big oak chest in the vaults under Stokesay Castle, and when either of them wanted any of it he just took the key and got some. But one day one of them wanted the key, and the other had got it, so he shouted to him to throw it over as they had been in the habit of doing, and he went to throw it, but somehow he made a mistake and threw too short, and dropped the key into the moat down by the Castle, where it has remained ever since. And the chest of treasure stands in the vaults still, but no one can approach it, for there is a big raven always sitting on the top of it, and he won't allow anybody to try and break it open, so no one will ever be able to get the giants' treasure until the key is found, and many say it never will be found, let folks try as much as they please."[53]

Amongst further reasons for the hiding away of money, may be noticed eccentricity of character, or mental delusion, a singular instance of which occurred some years ago. It appears that whilst some workmen were grubbing up certain tree at Tufnell Park, near Highgate, they came upon two jars, containing nearly four hundred pounds in gold. This they divided, and shortly afterwards, when the lord of the manor claimed the whole as treasure trove, the real owner suddenly made his appearance. In the course of inquiry, it transpired that he was a brassfounder, living at Clerkenwell, and having been about nine months before under a temporary delusion, he one night secreted the jars in a field at Tufnell Park. On proving the truth of his statement, the money was refunded to him.

FOOTNOTES:

[52] "Journal of the Archæological Association," 1859, Vol. xv., p. 104.

[53] "Shropshire Folklore" (Miss Jackson), 7, 8.

CHAPTER XVI.
LUCKY ACCIDENTS.

> "As the unthought-on accident is guilty
> Of what we wildly do, so we profess
> Ourselves to be the slaves of chance, and flies
> Of every wind that blows."
>
> "Winter's Tale," Act iv., Sc. 3.

Pascal, one day, remarked that if Cleopatra's nose had been shorter the whole face of the world would probably have been changed. The same idea may be applied to the unforeseen advantages produced by accidents, some of which have occasionally had not a little to do with determining the future position in life of many eminent men. Prevented from pursuing the sphere in this world they had intended, compulsory leisure compelled them to adopt some hobby as a recreation, in which, unconsciously, their real genius lay.

Thus David Allan, popularly known as the "Scottish Hogarth," owed his fame and success in life to an accident. When a boy, having burnt his foot, he amused the monotony of his leisure hours by drawing on the floor with a piece of chalk—a mode of passing his time which soon obtained an extraordinary fascination for him. On returning to school, he drew a caricature of his schoolmaster punishing a pupil, which caused him to be summarily expelled. But, despite this punishment, his success as an artist was decided, the caricature being considered so clever that he was sent to Glasgow to study art, where he was apprenticed in 1755 to Robert Foulis, a famous painter, who with his brother Andrew had secretly established an academy of arts in that city. Their kindness to him he was afterwards able to return when their fortunes were reversed.

If Sir Walter Scott had not sprained his foot in running round the room when a child, the world would probably have had none of those works which have made his name immortal. When his son intimated a desire to enter the army, Sir Walter Scott wrote to Southey, "I have no title to combat a choice which would have been my own, had not my lameness prevented." In the same way, the effects of a fall when about a year old rendered Talleyrand lame for life, and being, on this account, unfit for a military career, he was obliged to renounce his birthright in favour of his second brother. But what seemed an obstacle to his future success was the very reverse, for, turning his attention to politics and books, he eventually became one of the leading diplomatists of his day. Again, Josiah Wedgwood was seized in his boyhood with an attack of smallpox, which was followed by a disease in the right knee, some years afterwards necessitating the amputation of the affected limb. But, as Mr. Gladstone, in his address on Wedgwood's life and work delivered at Burslem, Oct. 26th, 1863, remarked, the disease from which he suffered was, no doubt, the cause of his subsequent greatness, for "it prevented him from growing up to be the active, vigorous English workman, but it put upon him considering whether, as he could not be that, he might not be something else, and something greater. It drove him to meditate upon the laws and secrets of his art."

Flamsteed was an astronomer by accident. Being removed from school on account of his health, it appears that a cold caught in the summer of 1660 while bathing, which produced a rheumatic affection of the joints, accompanied by other ailments. He became unable to walk to school, and he finally left in May, 1662. His self-training now began, and Sacroborco's "De Sphæra" was lent to him, with the perusal of which he was so pleased that he forthwith commenced a course of astronomic studies. Accordingly, he constructed a rude quadrant and calculated a table of the sun's altitudes, pursuing his studies, as he said himself, "under the discouragement of friends, the want of health, and all other instructors, except his better genius."[54]

Alluding to accidents as sometimes developing greatness, Mr. Smiles remarks that Pope's satire was in a measure the outcome of his deformity; and Lord Byron's club foot, he adds, "had probably not a little to do with determining his destiny as a poet. Had not his mind been embittered, and made morbid by his deformity, he might never have written a line. But his misshapen foot stimulated his mind, roused his ardour, threw him upon his own resources, and we know with what result."

Again, in numerous other ways, it has been remarked, accidents have taken a lucky turn, and, if not being the road to fortune, have had equally important results. The story is told of a young officer in the army of General Wolfe who was supposed to be dying of an abscess in the lungs. He was absent from his regiment on sick leave, but resolved to join it when a battle was expected, "for," said he, "since I am given over I had better be doing my duty, and my life's being shortened a few days matters not." He received a shot which pierced the abscess and made an opening for the discharge, the result being that he recovered and lived to eighty years of age.

Brunel, the celebrated engineer, had a curious accident, which might have forfeited his life. While one day playing with his children and astonishing them by passing a half sovereign through his mouth out at his ear, he unfortunately swallowed the coin, which dropped into his windpipe. Brunel regarded the mischief caused by the accident as purely mechanical; a foreign body had got into his breathing apparatus, and must be removed, if at all, by some mechanical expedient. But he was equal to the emergency, and had an apparatus constructed which had the effect of relieving him of the coin. In after days he used to tell how, when his body was inverted, and he heard the gold piece strike against his upper front teeth, was, perhaps, the most exquisite moment in his whole life, the half sovereign having been in his windpipe for not less than six weeks.

In the year 1784, William Pitt almost fell the victim to the folly of a festive meeting, for he was nearly accidentally shot as a highwayman. Returning late at night on horseback from Wimbledon to Addiscombe, together with Lord Thurlow, he found the turnpike gate between Tooting and Streatham thrown open. Both passed through it, regardless of the threats of the turnpike man, who, taking the two for highwaymen, discharged the contents of his blunderbuss at their backs; but, happily, no injury was done, and Pitt had the good fortune to escape from what might have been a very serious, if not fatal, accident. Foote, too, met with a bad accident on horseback, which, at the time, seemed a lasting obstacle to his career as an actor. Whilst riding with the Duke of York and some other noblemen, he was thrown from his horse and his leg broken, so that an amputation became necessary. In consequence of this accident, the Duke of York obtained for him the patent of the Haymarket Theatre for his life; but he continued to perform his former characters with no less agility and spirit than he had done before to the most crowded houses. Similarly, on one occasion—a very important one—Charles James Matthews was nearly prevented making his first appearance on the stage through being thrown from his horse, but, to quote his own words, "the excitement of the evening dominated all other feelings, and I walked for the time as well as ever."

Some men, again, have owed their success to the accidents of others. A notable instance was that of Baron Ward, the well-known minister of the Duke of Parma. After working some time as a stable-boy in Howden, he went to London, where he had the good luck to come to the Duke of Parma's assistance after a fall from his horse in Rotten Row. The Duke took him back to Lucca as his groom, and ere long Ward made the ducal stud the envy of Italy. He soon rose to a higher position, and became the minister and confidential friend of the Duke of Parma, with whom he escaped in the year 1848 to Dresden, and for whom he succeeded in recovering Parma and Placenza. Indeed, Lord Palmerston once remarked, "Baron Ward was one of the most remarkable men I ever met with."

It was through witnessing an accident that Sir Astley Cooper made up his final decision to take up surgery as his profession. A young man, having been run over by a cart, was in danger of dying from loss of blood, when young Cooper lost no time in tying his handkerchief about the wounded limb so as to stop the hemorrhage. It was this incident which assured him of his taste for surgery. In the same way, the story is quoted of the eminent French surgeon, Ambrose Paré. It is stated that he was acting as stable-boy to an abbé at Laval when a surgical operation was about to be performed on one of the brethren of the monastery. On being called in to assist, Ambrose Paré not only proved so useful, but was so fascinated with the operation that he made up his mind to devote his life to the study and practice of surgery. Instances of this kind might be enumerated, being of frequent occurrence in biographical literature, and showing to what unforeseen circumstances men have occasionally owed their greatness.

A romance which, had it lacked corroborative evidence, would have seemed highly improbable, is told of the two Countesses of Kellie. In the latter half of the last century, Mr Gordon, the proprietor of Ardoch Castle—situated upon a high rock, overlooking the sea—was one evening aroused by the firing of a gun evidently from a vessel in distress near the shore. Hastening down to the beach, with the servants of the Castle, it was evident that the distressed vessel had gone down, as the floating spars but too clearly indicated. After looking out in vain for some time, in the hope of recovering some of the passengers—either dead or alive—he found a sort of crib, which had been washed ashore, containing a live infant. The little creature proved to be a female child, but beyond the fact that its wrappings pointed to its being the offspring of persons in no mean condition, there was no trace as to who these were.

The little foundling was brought up with Mr. Gordon's own daughters, and when she had attained to womanhood, by an inexplicable coincidence, a storm similar to that just mentioned occurred. An alarm-gun was fired, and this time Mr. Gordon had the satisfaction of receiving a shipwrecked party, whom he at once made his guests at the Castle. Amongst them was one gentleman passenger, who after a comfortable night spent in the Castle, was surprised at breakfast by the entrance of a troop of blooming girls, the daughters of his host, as he understood, but one of whom specially attracted his attention.

"Is this young lady your daughter, too?" he inquired of Mr. Gordon.

"No," replied his host, "but she is as dear to me as if she were."

He then related her history, to which the stranger listened with eager interest, and at its close he not a little surprised Mr. Gordon by remarking that he "had reason to believe that the young lady was his own niece." He then gave a detailed account of his sister's return from India, corresponding to the time of the shipwreck, and added, "she is now an orphan, but if I am not mistaken in my supposition, she is entitled to a handsome provision which her father bequeathed to her in the hope of her yet being found."

Before many days had elapsed, sufficient evidence was forthcoming to prove that by this strange, but lucky, accident of the shipwreck, the long lost niece was found. The young heiress keenly felt leaving the old castle, but to soften the wrench it was arranged that one of the Misses Gordon should accompany her to Gottenburg, where her uncle had long been settled as a merchant.

The sequel of this romance, as it is pointed out in the "Book of Days,"[55] is equally astonishing. It seems that among the Scotch merchants settled in the Swedish port, was Mr. Thomas Erskine—a younger son of a younger brother of Sir William Erskine, of Cambo, in Fife—an offshoot of the family of the Earl of Kellie—to whom Miss Anne Gordon was married in the year 1771. A younger brother, named Methven, ten years later married Joanna, a sister of Miss Gordon. It was never contemplated that these two brothers would ever come near to the peerage of their family—there being at one time seventeen persons between them and the family titles; but in the year 1797 the baronet of Cambo became Earl of Kellie, and two years later the title came to the husband of Anne Gordon. In short, "these two daughters of Mr. Gordon, of Ardoch, became in succession Countesses of Kellie in consequence of the incident of the shipwrecked foundling, whom their father's humanity had rescued from the waves."

FOOTNOTES:

[54] See "Dictionary of National Biography," xix., 242.

[55] "The Two Countesses of Kellie," ii. 41, 42.

CHAPTER XVII.
FATAL PASSION.

> What dreadful havoc in the human breast
> The passions make, when, unconfined and mad,
> They burst, unguided by the mental eye,
> The light of reason, which, in various ways,
> Points them to good, or turns them back from ill!
>
> THOMSON.

The annals of some of our old and respected families have occasionally been sadly stained "by hideous exhibitions of cruelty and lust," in certain instances the result of an unscrupulous disregard of moral duty and of a vindictive fierceness in avenging injury. It has been oftentimes remarked that few tragedies which the brain of the novelist has depicted have surpassed in their unnatural and horrible details those enacted in real life, for

When headstrong passion gets the reins of reason,The force of Nature, like too strong a gale,For want of ballast, oversets the vessel.

Love, indeed, which has been proverbially said to lead to as much evil as any impulse that agitates the human bosom, must be held responsible for only too many of those crimes which from time to time outrage society, for, as the authors of "Guesses at Truth" have remarked, "jealousy is said to be the offspring of love, yet, unless the parent make haste to strangle the child, the child will not rest till it has poisoned the parent." Thus, a tragedy which made the Castle of Corstorphine the scene of a terrible crime and scandal in the year 1679, may be said to have originated in an unhallowed passion.

George, first Lord Forrester, having no male issue, made an arrangement whereby his son-in-law, James Baillie, was to succeed him as second Lord Forrester and proprietor of the estate of Corstorphine. Just four years after this compact was made, Lord Forrester died, and James Baillie, a young man of twenty-five, succeeded to the title and property. But this arrangement did not meet with the approval of Lord Forrester's daughters, who regarded it as a manifest injustice that the honours of their ancient family should devolve on an alien—a feeling of dissatisfaction which was more particularly nourished by the third daughter, Lady Hamilton, whose husband was far from wealthy.

It so happened that Lady Hamilton had a daughter, Christian, who was noted for her rare beauty and high spirit. But, unfortunately, she was a girl of strong passion, which, added to her self-will, caused her, when she had barely arrived at a marriageable age, to engage herself to one James Nimmo, the son of an Edinburgh merchant. Before many weeks had elapsed, the young couple were married, and the handsome young wife was settled in her new home in Edinburgh. Time wore on, the novelty of marriage died away, and as Mrs. Nimmo dwelt on her mercantile surroundings, she recognised more and more what an ill-assorted match she had made, and in her excitable mind, "she cursed the bond which connected her with a man whose social position she despised, and whose occupations she scorned." The report, however, of her uncommon beauty, could not fail to reach the ears of young Lord Forrester, who on the score of relationship was often attracted to Mrs. Nimmo's house. At first he was received with coldness, but, by flattering and appealing to her vanity, he gradually "accomplished the ruin of this unhappy young woman," and made her the victim of his licentious and unprincipled designs.

But no long time had elapsed when this shameful intrigue became the subject of common talk, and public indignation took the side of the injured woman, when Lord Forrester, after getting tired of her, "was so cruel and base as to speak of her openly in the most opprobrious manner," even alluding to her criminal connection with him. In so doing, however, he had not taken into consideration the violent character of the woman he had wronged, nor thought he of her jealousy, wounded pride, and despair. In his haste, also, to rid himself of the woman who no longer fascinated him, he paid no heed to the passion that was lurking in her inflamed bosom, nor counted on her spretæ injuria formæ.

On the other hand, whilst he was forgetting the past in his orgies, Mrs. Nimmo—whose love for him was turned to the bitterest hate—was hourly reproaching him, and at last the fatal moment arrived when she felt bound to proceed to Corstorphine Castle, and confront her evil-doer. At the time, Lord Forrester was drinking at the village tavern, and, when the infuriated woman demanded to see him, he was flushed with claret, and himself in no amiable mood. The altercation, naturally, "soon became violent, bitter reproaches were uttered on the one side, and contemptuous sneers on the other." Goaded to frenzy, the unhappy woman stabbed her paramour to the heart, killing him instantly.

When taken before the sheriff of Edinburgh, she confessed her crime, and, although she told the court in the most pathetic manner how basely she had been wronged by one who should have supported rather than ruined her, sentence of death was passed upon her. She managed, writes Sir Bernard Burke,[56] to postpone the execution of her sentence by declaring that she was with child by her seducer, and during her imprisonment succeeded in escaping in the disguise of a young man. But she was captured, and on the 12th November, 1679, paid the penalty of her rash act, appearing at her execution attired in deep mourning, covered with a large veil.

Radcliffe to this day possesses the tradition of a terrible tragedy of which there are several versions. It appears that one Sir William de Radclyffe had a very beautiful daughter whose mother died in giving her birth. After a time he married again, and the step-mother, actuated by feeling of jealousy, conceived a violent hatred to the girl, which ere long prompted her to be guilty of the most insane cruelty. One day, runs the story, when Sir William was out hunting, she sent the unsuspecting girl into the kitchen with a message to the cook that he was to dress the white doe. But the cook professing ignorance of the particular white doe he was to dress, asserted, to the young lady's intense horror, that he had received orders to kill her, which there and then he did, afterwards making her into a pie.

On Sir William's return from hunting, he made inquiries for his daughter, but his wife informed him that she had taken the opportunity in his absence of going into a nunnery. Suspicious, however, of the truth of her story—for her jealous hatred of his daughter had not escaped his notice—he flew into a passion, and demanded in the most peremptory manner where his daughter was, whereupon the scullion boy denounced the step-mother, and warned Sir William against eating the pie.

The whole truth was soon revealed, and the diabolic wickedness of Lady William did not pass unpunished, for she was burnt, and the cook was condemned to stand in boiling lead. A ballad in the Pepys' collection, entitled, "The Lady Isabella's Tragedy, or the Step-mother's Cruelty," records this horrible barbarity; and in a Lancashire ballad, called "Fair Ellen of Radcliffe", it is thus graphically told:—

She straighte into the kitchen went,Her message for to tell;And then she spied the master cook,Who did with malice swell.

"Nowe, master cooke, it must be soe,Do that which I thee tell;You needs must dress the milk-white doe,You which do knowe full well."

Then straight his cruel, bloody hands,He on the ladye laid,Who, quivering and ghastly, standsWhile thus to her he sayd:

"Thou art the doe that I must dress;See here! behold, my knife!For it is pointed, presentliTo rid thee of thy life."

O then, cryed out the scullion boye,As loud as loud might be,"O save her life, good master cook,And make your pyes of me."

The tradition adds that Sir William was not unmindful of the scullion boy's heroic conduct, for he made him heir to his possessions.

Another cruel case of woman's jealousy, which, happily, was not so disastrous in its result as the former, relates to Maria, daughter of the Hon. Alexander Mackenzie, second son of Kenneth, Earl of Seaforth, who was Maid of Honour to Queen Caroline. Report goes that between this young lady, who was one of the greatest beauties about the Court, and a Mr. Price, an admired man about town, there subsisted a strong attachment. Unfortunately for Miss Mackenzie, Mr. Price was an especial favourite of the celebrated Countess of Deloraine, who, to get rid of her rival in beauty, poisoned her.

But this crime was discovered in time, antidotes were administered with success, and the girl's life was saved; although her lovely complexion is said to have been ruined, ever after continuing of a lemon tint. Queen Caroline, desirous of shielding the Countess of Deloraine from the consequences of her act, persuaded "the poisoned beauty" to appear, as soon as she was sufficiently recovered, at a supper, given either by the Countess of Deloraine or where she was to be present. Accordingly, on the night arranged, some excitement was caused by the arrival of Miss Mackenzie, for as she entered the room, someone exclaimed, "How entirely changed!"

But Mr. Price, who was seated by Lady Deloraine remarked, "In my eyes she is more beautiful than ever," and it only remains to add that they were married next morning.

Like jealousy, thwarted love has often been cause of the most unnatural crimes, and a tragic story is told of the untimely death of Mr Blandy, of Henley, in Oxfordshire, who, by practice as an attorney, had accumulated a large fortune. He had an only child, Mary, who was regarded as an heiress, and consequently had suitors many. On one occasion, it happened that William Cranstoun, brother of Lord Cranstoun, being upon a recruiting party in Oxfordshire, and hearing of Miss Blandy's "great expectations," found an opportunity of introducing himself to the family.

The Captain's attentions, however, to Miss Blandy met with the strong disapproval of her father, for he had ascertained that this suitor for his daughter's hand had been privately married in Scotland. But against this objection Captain Cranstoun replied that he hoped to get this marriage speedily set aside by a decree of the Supreme Court of Session. And when the Court refused to annul the marriage, Mr. Blandy absolutely refused to allow his daughter to have any further communications with so dishonourable a man; a resolution to which he remained inexorable.

Intrigue between the two was the result, for it seems that Miss Blandy's affection for this profligate man—almost double her age—was violent. As might be expected, Captain Cranstoun not only worked upon her feelings, but imposed on her credulity. He sent her from Scotland a pretended love powder, which he enjoined her to administer to her father, in order to gain his affection and procure his consent. This injunction she did not carry out, on account of a frightful dream, in which she saw her father fall from a precipice into the ocean. Thereupon the Captain wrote a second time, and told her in words somewhat enigmatical, but easily understood by her, his design.

Horrible to relate, the wicked girl was so elated with the idea of removing her father, that she was heard to exclaim before the servants, "who would not send an old fellow to hell for thirty thousand pounds?"

The fatal die was cast. The deadly powder was mixed and given to him in a cup of tea, after drinking which he soon began to swell enormously.

"What have you given me, Mary?" asked the unhappy dying man. "You have murdered me; of this I was warned, but, alas! I thought it was a false alarm. O, fly; take care of the Captain!"

Thus Mr. Blandy died of poison, but his daughter was captured whilst attempting to escape, and was conveyed to Oxford Castle, where she was imprisoned till the assizes, when she was tried for parricide, was found guilty, and executed. Captain Cranstoun managed to effect his escape, and went abroad, where he died soon afterwards in a deplorable state of mind, brought about by remorse for the evil and misery he had caused.

Almost equally tragic was the fatal passion of Sir William Kyte, forming another strange domestic drama in real life. Possessed of considerable fortune, and of ancient family, Sir William was deemed a very desirable match, and when he offered his hand to a young lady of noble rank, and of great beauty, he was at once accepted. The marriage for the first few years turned out happily, but the crisis came when Sir William was nominated, at a contested election, to represent the borough of Warwick, in which county lay the bulk of his estate. After the election was over, Lady Kyte, by way of recompensing a zealous partisan of her husband, took an innkeeper's daughter, Molly Jones, for her maid; "a tall, genteel girl, with a fine complexion, and seemingly very modest and innocent." But before many months had elapsed, Sir William was attracted by the girl, and, eventually, became so infatuated by her charms, that, casting aside all restraints of shame or fear, he agreed to a separation between his wife and himself. Accordingly, Sir William left Lady Kyte, with the two younger children, in possession of the mansion-house in Warwickshire, and retired with his mistress and his two eldest sons to a farmhouse on the Cotswold hills. Charmed with the situation, he was soon tempted to build a handsome house here, to which were added two large side-fronts, for no better reason than that Molly Jones, one day, happened to say, "What is a Kite without wings." But the expense of completing this establishment, amounting to at least £10,000, soon involved Sir William in financial difficulties, which caused him to drown his worries in drink.

At this juncture, Molly Jones, forgetting her own past, was injudicious enough to engage a fresh coloured country girl—who was scarcely twenty—as dairymaid, for whom Sir William quickly conceived an amorous regard. Actuated by jealousy or disgust, Molly Jones threatened to leave Sir William, a resolution which she soon carried out, retiring to Cambden, a neighbouring market town, where she was reduced to keep a small sewing school as a means of livelihood. Although left to carry on his intrigue undisturbed, Sir William soon became a victim to gloomy reflections, feeling at times that he had not only cruelly wronged a good wife, but had been deserted by the very woman for whose sake he had brought this trouble and disgrace upon his family. Tormented by these conflicting passions, he occasionally worked himself up into such a state of frenzy that even his new favourite was terrified, and had run away. It was when almost maddened with the thought of his evil past that he formed that fatal resolve which was a hideous ending to "the dreadful consequence of a licentious passion not checked in its infancy." One October evening, as a housemaid was on the stairs, suddenly "the lobby was all in a cloud of smoke." She gave the alarm, and on the door being forced open whence the smoke proceeded, it was discovered that Sir William had set fire to a large heap of fine linen, piled up in the middle of the room. From an adjoining room, where Sir William had made his escape, the flames burst out with such fury that all were glad to make their escape out of the house, the greater part of which was in a few hours burnt to the ground—no other remains of its master being found next morning but the hip-bone, and bones of the back.

A case which, at the time, created considerable sensation was the murder of Thynne of Longleat by a jealous antagonist. The eleventh Duke of Northumberland left an only daughter, whose career, it has been said, "might match that of the most erratic or adventurous of her race." Before she was sixteen years old, she had been twice a widow, and three times a wife. At the age of thirteen, she was married to the only son of the Duke of Newcastle, a lad of her own age, who died in a few months. Her second husband was Thynne of Longleat, "Tom of Ten Thousand," but the tie was abruptly severed by the bullet of an assassin, set on by the notorious Count Konigsmark, who had been a suitor for her hand, and was desirous of another chance. After his death, the young widow, who was surrounded by a host of admirers, married the Duke of Somerset, and she seems to have made him a fitting mate, for when his second wife, a Finch, tapped him familiarly on the shoulder, or, according to another version, seated herself on his knee, he exclaimed indignantly:

"My first wife was a Percy, and she never thought of taking such a liberty."

It may be added that one of the most remarkable incidents in this celebrated beauty's life was when by dint of tears and supplications she prevented Queen Anne from making Swift a bishop, out of revenge for the "Windsor prophecy," in which she was ridiculed for the redness of her hair, and upbraided as having been privy to the brutal murder of her second husband. "It was doubted," says Scott, "which imputation she accounted the more cruel insult, especially since the first charge was undoubted, and the second arose only from the malice of the poet."

Another tragedy of a similar kind was the murder of William Mountford, the player. Captain Richard Hill had conceived a violent passion for Mrs. Bracegirdle, the beautiful actress, and is said to have offered her his hand, and to have been refused. At last his passion became ungovernable, and he determined to carry her off by force. To carry out his purpose, he induced his friend Lord Mohun to assist him in the attempt. According to one account, "he dodged the fair actress for a whole day at the theatre, stationed a coach near the Horseshoe Tavern, in Drury Lane, to carry her off in, and hired six soldiers to force her into it. As the beautiful actress came down Drury Lane, at ten o'clock at night, accompanied by her mother and brother, and escorted by her friend Mr. Page, one of the soldiers seized her in his arms, and endeavoured to force her into the coach. But the lady's scream attracted a crowd, and Captain Hill, finding his endeavours ineffectual, bid the soldiers let her go. Disappointed in their object, Lord Mohun and Captain Hill vowed vengeance; and Mrs. Bracegirdle on reaching home sent her servant to Mr. Mountford's house to take care of himself, warning him against Lord Mohun and Captain Hill, "who she feared, had no good intention toward him, and did wait for him in the street." It appears that Mountford had already heard of the attempt to carry off Mrs. Bracegirdle, and hearing that Lord Mohun and Captain Hill were in the street, did not shrink from approaching them."

The account says that he addressed Lord Mohun, and told him how sorry he was to find him in the company of such a pitiful fellow as Captain

Hill, whereupon, it is said, "the captain came forth and said he would justify himself, and went towards the middle of the street, and Mr. Mountford followed him and drew." The end of the quarrel was that Mountford fell with a terrible wound, of which he died on the following day, declaring in his last moments that Captain Hill ran him through the body before he could draw his sword. Captain Hill, it seems, owed Mountford a deadly grudge, having attributed his rejection by Mrs. Bracegirdle to her love for him—an unlikely passion, it is thought, as Mountford was a married man, with a good-looking wife of his own, afterwards Mrs. Verbruggen, and a celebrated actress.

Oulton House, Suffolk, long known as the "Haunted House," acquired its ill-omened name from a tragic occurrence traditionally said to have happened many years ago, and the peasantry in the neighbourhood affirm that at midnight a wild huntsman, with his hounds, accompanied by a lady carrying a poisoned cup, is occasionally seen. The story is that, in the reign of George II., a squire, returning unexpectedly home from the chase, discovered his wife with an officer, one of his guests, in too familiar a friendship. High words followed, and the indignant husband, provoked by the cool manner in which the officer treated the matter, struck him, whereupon the guilty lover drew his sword and drove it through the squire's heart, the faithless wife and her paramour afterwards making their escape.

Some years afterwards, runs the tale, the Squire's daughter, who had been left behind in the hasty departure, having grown to womanhood, was affianced to a youthful farmer of the neighbourhood. But on their bridal eve, as they were sitting together talking over the new life they were about to enter, "a carriage, black and sombre as a hearse, with closely drawn curtains, and attended by servants clad in sable liveries, drew up to the door." The young girl was seized by masked men, carried off in the carriage to her unnatural mother, while her betrothed was stabbed as he vainly endeavoured to rescue her. A grave is pointed out in the cemetery at Namur, as that in which was laid the body of the unhappy girl, poisoned, it is alleged, by her unscrupulous and wicked mother. It is not surprising, we are told, that the locality was supposed to be haunted by the wretched woman—both as wife and mother equally criminal.

Family romance, once more, has many a dark page recording how despairing love has ended in self-destruction. At the beginning of the present century, a sad catastrophe befell the Shuckburghs of Shuckburgh Hall. It appears the Bedfordshire Militia were stationed near Upper Shuckburgh, and the officers were in the habit of visiting the Hall, whose hospitable owner, Sir Stewkley Shuckburgh, received them with every mark of cordiality. His daughter, then about twenty years of age, was a young lady of no ordinary attractions, and her fascinations soon produced their natural effect on one of the officers, Lieutenant Sharp, who became deeply attached to her. But as soon as Sir Stewkley became aware of this love affair, he gave it his decided disapproval. Lieutenant Sharp was forbidden the house, and Miss Shuckburgh resolved to smother her love in deference to her father's wishes. It was accordingly decided between the young people that their intimacy should cease, and that the letters which had passed between them should be returned. An arrangement was, therefore, made that the lady should leave the packet for Lieutenant Sharp in the summer-house in the garden on a specified evening, and that on the following morning she should find the packet intended for her in the same place. The sad engagement was kept, and having left her packet in the evening, Miss Shuckburgh set out on the following morning to find her own. A servant, it is said, who saw her in the garden, was curious to know what could have brought her out at so early an hour. He followed her unobserved, and on drawing near to the summer-house, "he heard the voices of the lieutenant and of the lady in earnest dispute. The officer was loud and impassioned, the lady firm but unconsenting. Immediately was heard the report of a pistol, and the fall of a body—another report and fall. Guessing the tragic truth, the servant raised an alarm, and the two lovers were found lying dead in their own blood." It is generally supposed that this terrible act of self-destruction was the result of mutual agreement—the outcome of passion and despair.

"Since that hour," writes Howitt, "every object, about the place which could suggest to the memory this fatal event, has been changed or removed. The summer-house has been razed to the ground; the disposition of the garden itself altered; but," he adds, "such tragic passages in human life become part and parcel of the scene where they occur—they become the topic of the winter fireside. They last while passions and affections, youth and beauty last. They fix themselves into the soil, and the very rock on which it lies, and though the house was razed from the spot, and its park and pleasaunces turned into ploughed fields, it would still be said for ages: Here stood Shuckburgh Hall, and here fell the young and lovely Miss Shuckburgh by the hand of her despairing lover."

And to conclude with a romance in brief, some forty or fifty years ago, in the far north of England a girl was on the eve of being married. Her wedding dress was ordered, the guests were bidden. But, it is said that at the eleventh hour, in a fit of passion and paltry jealousy, she resented some fancied want of devotion in her lover.

He was single-minded, loyal, and altogether of finer stuff than herself; but she was a wretched slave to such old sk phrases as delicacy, family pride, and the like, and so he was allowed to go, for she came of people who looked upon unforgiveness as a virtue.

Accordingly the discarded lover exchanged into a regiment under orders for Afghanistan. At the time, our troops were engaged there in hot fighting. The lad fell, and hidden on his breast was found a locket which his sweetheart had once given him. It came back to her through a brother officer, who had known something of his sad story, with a stain on it—a stain of his blood. When that painful relic silently told her of the devotion which she had so unjustly and basely wronged, there came, in the familiar lines:

A mist and a weeping rain,And life was never the same again.

That stain marked every day of a lonely life throughout forty years or more.

FOOTNOTES:

[56] "Vicissitudes of Families," 1863, III. Ser., 202-203.

Milton Keynes UK
Ingram Content Group UK Ltd.
UKHW030957261124
451585UK00005B/667